How To Go On

LIVING

After the Death of a Baby

LARRY G. PEPPERS, Ph.D.
RONALD J. KNAPP, Ph.D.

PEACHTREE PUBLISHERS LIMITED
Atlanta, Georgia

129825

Published by
PEACHTREE PUBLISHERS, LTD.
494 Armour Circle, N.E.
Atlanta, Georgia 30324

Manufactured in the United States of America

First printing

Library of Congress Catalog Number 85-060338

ISBN: 0-931948-69-X

Portions of this material originally appeared in
Motherhood & Mourning/Perinatal Death, copyright
1980 by Praeger Publishers.

Cover design by Paulette Lambert

Photograph by Lea Laseter

How To Go On

LIVING

After the Death of a Baby

ABOUT THE AUTHORS

LARRY G. PEPPERS is an Associate Professor of Sociology at Clemson University, Clemson, South Carolina. He teaches courses in Marriage and the Family, the Sociology of Aging, and Social Psychology.

Dr. Peppers has published articles in such journals as *Psychiatry*, *The Journal of Medical Education*, *The Gerontologist*, *The Journal of Drug Issues*, and others.

Dr. Peppers holds a B.S. and M.S. from Memphis State University and a Ph.D. from Oklahoma State University.

RONALD J. KNAPP is Professor of Sociology at Clemson University, Clemson, South Carolina. He teaches courses in the Sociology of Death, Population, and the Family.

Dr. Knapp has published in a variety of journals, including *Psychological Bulletin*, *The Journal of Applied Psychology*, *The Journal of Drug Issues*, *Psychiatry*, and *The Journal of Medical Education*. Dr. Knapp has another book, *Beyond Endurance: Coping With the Death of a Child*, Schocken Books, forthcoming in 1985.

Dr. Knapp holds a B.A. from Albion College, Albion, Michigan, and an M.A. from Bowling Green State University. His Ph.D. is from The Ohio State University.

PREFACE

We are frequently asked how two male sociologists got involved in studying maternal grief. This is like asking two veterans about their war experiences; we never tire of answering, for the issue is both professional and personal to us.

A few years ago, we were doing a series of death attitude studies, a natural outgrowth of our teaching areas, the Sociology of Aging and the Sociology of Death. We had paid little attention to death among the young until one of our wives, much interested in our research, began to discuss with us the emotional difficulties she had had after a stillbirth. The problem, as she identified it, is that usually only the mother knows the child really well and is thus left to bear her grief in near isolation.

As she discussed her feelings, she defined our present work. And we began a search for a group of mothers who had experienced fetal/infant death. We found that group through AMEND (Aid to Mothers Experiencing Neonatal Death), an organization located in St. Louis. With the cooperation of AMEND, we were able to arrange interviews with forty-two mothers who had lost neonates.

We were totally unprepared for what we encountered. It quickly became apparent that we were not dealing with simple interrelationships of variables or statistics but rather with a series of complex, sensitive, highly emotional, and heartrending stories of human tragedy.

The preliminary summary of our findings was reported in a United Press International news release. Response to the release was astounding. We received hundreds of lengthy letters from women throughout the world describing their own experiences with infant death and volunteering to participate in our research. Many of them completed questionnaires for us, and we interviewed others. From the letters, questionnaires, and interviews, we have developed a broad and detailed picture of the problems grieving mothers face.

Our study has four main purposes. First, we want to stimulate an awareness of the tragedy of fetal/infant death. Few of us recognize the extent of this problem or the devastating effects it has on the surviving parents, especially on the mothers. Second, we hope that our account and analysis of a large number of actual cases will help other parents who lose infants understand the normalcy of their feelings, helping them cope as they realize they are not alone. At the same time, we hope our work will alert families and friends to the significance of infant loss to the mother and direct them to supportive interactions with her. Finally, this book should serve as a practical guide to professionals — counselors, psychologists, psychiatrists, nurses, physicians, social workers — who interact with these mothers at the time of loss and throughout the grief process.

It would be presumptuous for us to claim that this book will provide answers to all questions and solutions for all problems that a grieving mother faces. We do believe, however, that many of her questions and problems might be resolved if she has an understanding of the grief process, an understanding of the attitude toward infant death in our society, and a realization that other women, many other women, are sharing the same questions and problems. To this end we hope that the reader will find this book beneficial.

Our heartfelt appreciation goes to all the parents who recounted their experiences to us. They provided us with not only the basic content of this book (every quotation is actual), but they also deeply touched our own emotions.

Several other individuals were instrumental in the completion of the manuscript. We thank Sister Jane Marie, Dr. Jim Menke, Sister Brigid Hirschfield, Hazelanne Lewis, Dr. Gary Sherman, Dr. Robert Henningsen and the Clemson University Faculty Research Committee, Michelle White, Lois Driver, Wayne Heath,

Pat McCormick, Maureen Connelly, and Robyn Altman.

We make grateful acknowledgment to SHARE, AMEND, and The Compassionate Friends for material about support groups found in the final sections. We also thank *The American Funeral Director* and *The Journal of Medical Education* for permission to adapt our previously published articles for inclusion in this book.

Larry G. Peppers, Ph.D.
Ronald J. Knapp, Ph.D.
Clemson, South Carolina

The Problem Is Real

LISA AND TODD

Lisa and Todd were not disappointed to learn that in seven months they would be parents. Sure, Lisa thought, the idea of being stigmatized as "having to get married" had crossed her mind; but after all, she was twenty-three and had been on her own for several years. She and Todd had planned to be married anyway, even prior to the news of the pregnancy. The surprising information simply advanced their timetable.

Their relationship had followed a nontraditional path. Lisa had graduated from college with a major in special education and, luckily, had had no trouble finding a teaching job in a private school for the mentally handicapped. She didn't know why, but these children seemed to have a special attachment to her. Her first-year evaluation noted, "Miss Simpson has an incredible affinity for relating to the children's special handicaps — they are all attracted to her."

Everyone who knew Lisa considered her to be the model "all-American girl," a petite brunette, healthy in mind, body, and soul. Lisa had consciously geared her lifestyle to perpetuate this image.

Graduation with honors from the University of Southern California had not marked an end to her studies. Despite the new responsibilities of her teaching career, Lisa, an avid reader, enrolled in graduate school. After a short year and a half she completed her master's degree and contemplated pursuing a doctorate, but because she felt further education would be detrimental to her immediate career, she decided to wait a year or two.

Although Lisa had been popular during her college days, her dedication to a career, coupled with a dearth of men in her profession, had greatly reduced her number of nights out. She had, however, maintained a close relationship with her college roommate and two of her fellow teachers, all of them married. They would often get together for dinner or lunch when her friends constantly talked of introducing her to "some guy you just have to meet!" It was not until she met Todd, a young attorney who had wandered into her classroom gathering information for a civic club speech, that she felt any desire for an involvement. During the following eleven months their relationship evolved from dinner on Saturday, to dinner three or four nights a week and tennis in the afternoon, to ski weekends, to discussion of marriage. Lisa remembers that "After the first few dates we both knew marriage was inevitable; the only question was 'how soon.'" The announcement was both expected and welcomed by family and friends.

Within a few months, she became pregnant. The pregnancy was a normal one with the exception of an unusually high weight gain. During the seventh month both Jane, her old roommate, and Mary, one of her fellow teachers, informed Lisa of their pregnancies. "Must be contagious," they laughed, and they spent the next two months together — shopping, attending baby showers, and having long discussions about plans, hopes, and dreams for their babies' futures. These were times of happy anticipation for all three women.

The thirty-eight pounds Lisa gained during pregnancy was of major concern to her and her obstetrician. When labor began twelve days early, she wanted to accept the encouraging words, "You're going to have a big, healthy one," but she harbored doubts. She knew that such an increase in weight was unusual, that it could be a problematic symptom of a diabetic mother.

The normal delivery of a ten-pound five-ounce boy diminished many of Lisa's anxieties. But when she was back in her room and recovering from sedation, Todd informed her, "He's a beautiful child, but there are some difficulties." The baby had been moved to the intensive care unit where treatment had begun for an enlarged heart and liver and a blood-sugar problem. Confident in herself, her son, and God, and encouraged by the hospital staff and pediatrician, who comforted her with soothing words like, "With every minute he lives, the odds of his recovery are greater," Lisa knew everything would work out well. She also knew the size of the baby was indicative of possible retardation, a thought which did not really concern her. As a result of the pleasure she had derived from her students, her thought was simply, "If a mother must have a handicapped child, let it be me."

Five days passed, and the words of encouragement from the staff continued — "With every minute he lives, his chances are greater." Lisa didn't know that her parents and Todd were hearing a different story; otherwise, she would have heeded their warnings of "prepare yourself for the worst." But, she thought, this was typical of their usual philosophical approach — expect the worst, and you can only be pleasantly surprised.

Lisa's feelings of frustration built during those five days. She felt a desperate need to see and hold her baby, but she was deprived of the opportunity. She remembered that feeding time was especially difficult — seeing the nurses carrying babies into and out of the other rooms. Her roommate, in the semiprivate room, also contributed to Lisa's unfortunate experience. She was a young, unmarried girl who informed Lisa of her plans to offer her baby for adoption. Feeling a growing hostility toward her, Lisa requested a move to another room. The nurse responded, "Honey, she's young and really doesn't mean what she's saying — your baby will be fine soon and you will feel better." Perhaps so, thought Lisa, but now when I feel such a need just to see my baby, she doesn't even want to feed hers.

She saw her baby, Jeffrey, for the first time when the priest baptized him. She recalls being strapped into a wheelchair and rolled to a window through which she could observe the ceremony. She watched as the priest put his hands through the portholes of the isolette and touched her son. The sight of Jeffrey merely heightened Lisa's desire to hold him. "It's just not fair," were her angry thoughts. "That priest is no more sanitary than I am. Why can't I touch him? Why can't I hold him?" Her wish was not to be fulfilled.

At 2:00 A.M. on the fifth morning, Lisa was awakened by the silent stirring of air in her room. A nurse informed her that she was being moved to another room, as she had requested. Realizing the unusual nature of these actions, Lisa panicked — "What's happened to my baby?" Again she was assured that everything was fine; another woman had been discharged and they were simply honoring her request to be moved. Lisa slept very little and could hardly wait until morning. At 8:00 A.M. she phoned Todd. No answer. "That's right, it's Sunday; he must be in church," she thought. She called again at 9:00 A.M., but there was still no answer. Her mind began to race. "Where is he? Why isn't he at home? In God's name, what is happening?" The nurses appeared stone-faced and would volunteer no information. The standard response was, "Everything is fine."

Lisa was nearly frantic when, at 10:00 in the morning, Todd walked into her room. The tears in his eyes and the strain on his face spoke the words that he quietly repeated: "We lost him: Jeffrey died last night."

"Oh God, no!" she cried. Her body began to quiver and a sick, nauseated feeling swept over her. She could only repeat, "Oh God, no!" Todd saw the pain in her face and the tears welled in his eyes. He could not contain himself; he began to cry. At that point Lisa broke down, and they wept together for their son.

The pain was excruciating. She said later that she never would have dreamed anyone could feel so much sorrow for someone so small and so young. How she managed to survive for the next few months under the terrible impact of her loss was something she does not yet fully understand. Her grief during the first days and weeks was overwhelming. She could hardly bring herself to function normally; and what was so disturbing to her was that her reactions seemed so out of proportion to the way others were reacting. Even Todd seemed to withdraw; he no longer displayed his feelings. It was as if the community said, "That's enough, we'll have no more grief. We'll have no more of this crying and carrying on!"

Under the recommendation that it was "best for her," the physician suggested that Lisa remain in the hospital for two more days. During that time she felt both grateful and relieved when her father volunteered to handle the funeral arrangements, alone and very quietly. She felt included when she was asked if there were any special baby clothes she wanted Jeffrey to wear. These feelings later turned to a quiet resentment when she learned that the funeral had been quite elaborate and that the decision had been made to exclude her, for "her own good." She felt hurt and angered when, the next morning, the volunteer Gray Lady cheerfully bounded into her room and greeted her with, "Well, how is this new mother today?"

Lisa also remembers those first few weeks after returning home — going from room to room crying, not being able to concentrate, trying to struggle through the day, being determined not to be excluded again, feeling resentment, anger, bitterness, self-pity, and guilt. She recalls the loneliness and self-imposed isolation from her friends. "After all, they are still pregnant; I don't want to scare them," were her thoughts. She also remembers the effect on her relationship with Todd.

Todd was strong throughout the ordeal. After several weeks Lisa began to have an intense desire to resume their sexual relationship, but her constant crying, which was now looked upon as totally inappropriate by family and friends, tended to evoke a comforting rather than a passionate response from Todd. She decided, therefore, that if they were to return to a normal life, the crying must stop. And so it did — after 4:00 P.M. (when Todd was home!). And so it went for seven or eight months.

Eventually Lisa accepted her loss, but for seven years she was not able to relate her feelings to any other person, not even to her husband. It simply wasn't possible in Lisa's mind that God was "punishing her" with Jeffrey's death. If not, then why? Why did he die? She realized she didn't even know the cause of death. Six years later, after months of requests, she finally was allowed to see the autopsy report. To her total surprise, she learned that the baby's heart was in fact normal, and so was the liver. Jeffrey had died, not from these causes, as the doctor had told her at the time, but according to the autopsy report, from an "experimental" medical procedure that had caused his lungs to fill with fluid. Todd's response to this information was, "My God, they killed our baby!" With that startling information after six long years, Todd grieved openly for the first time since that Sunday morning in Lisa's hospital room. This tragic piece of unexpected news opened the door to communication between Lisa and Todd, communication that had been closed for so long. It also reinstituted the close bonds between them that were present before Jeffrey's death. Today Lisa has resumed her teaching career and Todd is a partner in a successful law firm. They have never forgotten Jeffrey, or the anguish that followed his death. As time passes, they will be more able to come to terms with their loss. It will get easier. It always does.

VIRGINIA AND MICHAEL

The snowplows had yet to reach Brekenridge Drive as Virginia Johnson observed the many children who were enjoying both the playground created by last night's snowfall and their unexpected vacation from school. As she watched the snowballs fly, the sleds slowly inch down the sidewalk, and the slipping and falling of "little brother" trying to keep pace with "older brother," Virginia could hardly keep from thinking ahead to the time when her two sons would join this revelry in the street. James was already two-and-a-half and it seemed like only yesterday that she had brought

Barry home from the hospital. It just didn't seem possible that that had been eight months ago.

The past year had been a good one for the Johnson family. Michael had gotten a promotion, so for the first time home was a house rather than an apartment; then, during the middle of spring, Barry had arrived.

Barry's birth had not been easy. In fact, it had been a difficult pregnancy, and even with all the medications and treatment, Virginia had needed a hysterectomy. Despite the surgery, Virginia had taken it all in stride, for God had blessed them with the two healthy children they had planned.

And so December 10, 1971, began. With the exception of the somewhat unexpected snow and its inconveniences, it appeared to be just another day of preparation for the upcoming holidays. For Virginia and Michael Johnson, however, this would be a day they would never forget; they would soon experience an event that would literally overwhelm them for several years to come.

The day passed smoothly, despite James's six changes of clothes; and having completed her day of household chores, Virginia put the two boys to bed and retired to the bedroom with a good book. Michael, determined to finish the painting, and lacking only the foyer, decided to complete the job that night. Though the painting had been a long process, the finishing touches were finally in sight, and the shimmering snow outside made the work inside all the more pleasant.

As the clock struck midnight, Michael decided to take a short break. Down the hallway he could see that Virginia had fallen asleep with her book at her side. He entered the bedroom and turned the lights out; then he thought he heard a sound from the boys' room across the hall. He switched on the hallway light and peered in, but everything seemed to be in order. Both boys were sound asleep. James was rolled up in a fetal position and Barry was in his crib, lying on his stomach with a blanket covering all but his head. Perhaps he had heard a cough, or maybe James had bumped the wall with his arm. Everything looked fine and Michael took this moment to reflect on his accomplishments of the recent past and to consider the responsibilities of the future. The peaceful sight in front of him filled him with pride as he thought about the two healthy sons who would soon grow out of the infant stage and become images of himself.

With only one more wall to finish, Michael returned to his painting. Two hours later, the job completed, he decided to call it a day. As the prickly jets of water from the shower massaged him, Michael's thoughts turned to the upcoming visit of his in-laws and the many odds and ends that still needed to be completed before Christmas. If only his parents could visit, too. After he finished with his shower, Michael decided to check the boys one more time before turning in.

Again he turned on the hallway light and peered into their room. James had kicked his blanket down to his feet and then, instinctively, followed it. James was such an angel in his sleep, he thought, unlike the demanding and somewhat devilish child during his waking hours. As Michael moved his son to the top of the bed, he was struck by the bright calmness of the snow outside. He wondered if such sights were why young James had insisted on having his bed by the window.

Moving quietly across the room so as not to awaken the baby, Michael noticed that Barry was still lying on his stomach; but now the blanket was pulled over his head, and his left arm was hanging through the side of the crib. In the semidarkness Michael gently pulled the cover from Barry's head and attempted to move him to the center of the bed. As he lifted the baby, he noticed that Barry felt very limp; he turned him on his back and, with only the dim light from the hallway to aid him, knew immediately that something was wrong. He snatched the baby from the crib, ran quickly into the den, and laid him on the sofa under the lamp. It was then that he saw the paleness of Barry's face and the small trickle of blood from his nose. "Virginia! Virginia! Come here, hurry!" Michael called; and then immediately, perhaps on instinct, he began to administer mouth-to-mouth resuscitation.

Still half-asleep, Virginia, shocked by the sight in front of her, screamed, "My God, what happened?"

Michael replied, "I don't know, something bad!"

Shaken but fully awake, Virginia instinctively ran to the kitchen phone and dialed the number of the emergency medical service.

Within ten minutes a paramedic was working feverishly to restore the baby's breathing. Another was bombarding Michael with questions. "Did you drop the baby?" "Has anyone been ill lately?" "Is the baby taking any medication?"

Michael, half-dazed, could simply reply, "No, no, he had a checkup two days ago and was in perfect health."

"Why did you wait so long to call us?"

As Virginia watched the frantic scene, this last question, she noticed, seemed to convey a hint of accusation. Through the window she could see the flashing red lights. She also noticed windows lighted in the houses across the street. She heard a cry from the boys' room and found young James standing in his bed and crying as he looked at the unusual sights outside his window, sights so completely alien to the peaceful calmness of only an hour before. The phone began to ring and Mary, the next-door neighbor, was cautiously knocking at the front door.

Meanwhile, the paramedics continued their attempts to revive Barry. After what seemed an eternity, Virginia heard one of them say, "We've got to get to the hospital." Michael, tearless and silent, had withdrawn across the room, helplessly watching the nightmare in front of him.

If Michael had been thinking more clearly, he might have realized the gravity of the situation as he watched the emergency squad disconnect their monitoring apparatus, place his son on a gurney, and briskly roll him to the waiting ambulance. By this time several inquisitive neighbors had gathered outside, and Mary was checking with Virginia to see if there were any special instructions before she carried James to her house. "There is something wrong with the baby," Virginia said to one of the onlookers. "But I'm sure everything will be O.K." A few days in the hospital will make him better, Virginia reasoned to herself — she refused to believe what was actually happening. Climbing into the ambulance, she could still see the glazed look in Michael's eyes as he eased the car in behind them.

University Hospital was only five miles from 801 Brekenridge Drive, but the snow and the urgency made the usual ten-minute drive seem endless. So many disconnected thoughts raced through Virginia's mind as they made their way to the emergency room. Did I leave Mary a key to the house? Should I call Mom and Dad? I hope Michael doesn't hit an ice patch. What could have happened? Everything was O.K. when I went to bed. What did he mean by "Why did you wait so long to call?" Surely everything will be all right. Some of the best doctors in the country are waiting for us. Relax, she told herself, we're almost there.

Somehow, thought Virginia, the glimmering of the snow under the lights of the hospital and the silence of early morning provided the setting for a dream rather than a hospital full of human drama — the happiness of the new mothers on the maternity floor, the sadness of the terminally ill, the anxieties of waiting friends and relatives, and the many staff members, each with his own concerns. For Virginia and Michael, the brief stay there would become the most agonizing two hours that they would come to remember.

Barry had been rushed into the emergency room, and through the swinging doors of the treatment area. One of the nurses showed Virginia and Michael to a waiting area, and their vigil began. After only a few minutes, two uniformed police officers approached them. Explaining that it was "routine procedure" in emergency situations "like this," they began to ask a series of questions. When was he found? By whom? What happened? Surely they don't believe we caused Barry's problem!, Virginia thought to herself. But then, Michael does sound rather evasive. Why can't he say more than a simple, "I don't know." Well, evidently they have heard enough; thank God, they are leaving.

By 3:00 A.M. Virginia and Michael had convinced themselves that young Barry's problem was under control. They reasoned that he had been in the treatment room for thirty minutes, and they had yet to hear anything. The longer they waited, the more assured they became that their son had survived.

The worst thought — that Barry had not survived — was still totally denied. He will be O.K., they insisted. It was 3:20 A.M. before a doctor finally emerged through the swinging doors. Rather than give them an answer to their unasked question, he, too, began to question them. Who found Barry? What position was he in? How long did it take the rescue team to arrive? After about five minutes of such questions, with tears welling in his eyes, the physician ended their suspense: "I'm sorry," he said, "We could do nothing. Your son was dead when he arrived." For a brief moment, Michael and Virginia stood frozen in disbelief. Then their world collapsed as the harsh realization came crashing down on them that their baby, their youngest son, was dead — a victim, they later discovered, of Sudden Infant Death Syndrome (SIDS), a quiet killer that steals life from ten thousand to fifteen thousand babies every year.

For Michael and Virginia, that cold winter morning was the beginning of a prolonged period of bitterness, resentment, depression, anger, denial, and above all, guilt. During the subsequent twelve months Micheal began drinking heavily, and Virginia withdrew into an emotionless shell. Communication between them became more and more superficial and eventually ceased altogether. The joy of the new home changed to an atmosphere in which memories of death clouded everything. The Christmas gifts remained unopened.

One of the many tragedies of this story is that Michael and Virginia suffered alone, isolated from friends, neighbors, and relatives, who simply could not understand the depth of their feelings and their prolonged reactions to the death of an eight-month-old child. Five years later both recalled that the one pressing, yet unfulfilled, need they had during that time was to talk to someone about their feelings; however, when they brought up the topic, they were encouraged to forget, and certainly no one ever mentioned Barry's death to them. As a result they suffered three years of lonely, silent grief. Christmas has yet to be a happy occasion since that morning in December 1971. The irony of this account of Virginia and Michael Johnson is that they, to a certain extent, consider themselves lucky. Because the physicians at University Hospital were knowledgeable about Sudden Infant Death Syndrome, the Johnsons were spared continued interrogation and suspicion by the authorities. Other, totally innocent parents have not been so fortunate; some have spent time in jail, and many have suffered harrassment due to a lack of understanding and knowledge about this unexplained killer of infants. Virginia and Michael are beginning to overcome their grief. It has been a slow process, but they are becoming able to deal with their loss. They have recently started meeting with other parents who have experienced SIDS. They have come to realize that they are not alone.

Unfortunately for Lisa and Todd and Virginia and Michael, the actual deaths of their infants were only the beginning of a series of crucial events and decisions, each of which was to have an important impact on their mental health for years to come. Unlike the death of an older person, which is to some extent expected, the death of an infant is usually a surprise. As such, it leaves the parents with few guidelines and certainly precludes advance preparation. After months of anticipation and planning for their new arrival, they are suddenly faced with decisions and circumstances concerning death rather than life, grief rather than elation. Too many times it is their first encounter with death and its aftermath.

What did I do to cause the death? Should I see the child? Should I name the child? Why me, God? What about funeral arrangements? What did they do to my baby? Was he normal? What about the autopsy? These are only a few of the many questions that must be resolved by these parents within the first few hours after their loss. They search for answers to their questions during a time of shock and despair and in an atmosphere in which, regrettably, they find little, if any, support. For most bereaved parents, the grief will be shared with only a few other people. For many, the emotion and heartache will be borne alone. For some, the resolution of grief will take months, for others it will take years. But in all cases, the death of their baby will haunt them for many years; and because of this experience their lives will never be the same again.

MISCARRIAGES, STILLBIRTHS, INFANT DEATHS: WHAT DO WE KNOW?

The experiences of Lisa and Todd and Virginia and Michael are not unusual. They are shared by approximately 250,000 couples in the United States each year. Startling as it may seem, approximately one in three children conceived each year do not reach their first birthday.

These deaths all fall into one of the four major categories which comprise perinatal (fetal/infant) death: (1) those occurring within the first year of life from an as yet undetermined cause, Sudden Infant Death Syndrome; (2) those occurring during the first six months of life from some known cause, neonatal death; (3) stillbirth; and (4) those occurring during the prenatal period, miscarriage or spontaneous abortion.

While the United States ranks above other nations in technological knowledge, military might, food production, and economic standard of living, according to the World Health Organization it ranks fourteenth among nations in cases of infant mortality. Estimates reveal that some twelve thousand to fifteen thousand infants annually fall victim to Sudden Infant Death Syndrome, and over forty thousand succumb to neonatal death. In addition, about two out of every hundred pregnancies result in stillbirth and ten to twenty in miscarriage. Thus, despite the technological sophistication of the United States, perinatal death remains a significant occurrence. Even by the most conservative estimates, the actual number of fetal/infant deaths approaches 250,000 annually. While great strides are presently being made in obstetrics and neonatology, many parents are still beset with this tragedy.

Only within the past decade has the topic of death and dying emerged from its cultural taboo and become an area for scientific investigation and dialogue. Colleges and universities now offer credit for courses on this subject. The popular media have incorporated the death and dying storyline for movies and television productions, with such presentations as "Eric," "Sunshine," "Brian's Song," and *Terms of Endearment*. Although such factual and fictional presentations do not always depict the reality of death, they do represent significant departures from the silence of the past.

Perhaps this marks a positive advance in American society in the sense that the veil that has shrouded us from the topic of death for so long is being lifted and the subject of grief and bereavement is being approached in a more realistic and objective manner without the fear of negative reaction. Unfortunately, little attention has been given to the death of those who have had little opportunity for life — infants — and to those mothers who have experienced the tragedy of losing their babies. Their grief is, in many ways, unique and demanding of attention.

Each of us lives and each will die. We are born; we enjoy the careless days of childhood, the pleasures of parenthood and grand-parenthood; we endure the maladies of old age; and then we die. At least, these are the general expectations that most human beings hold. Death is viewed as a phenomenon of old age. We witness and grieve the loss of our parents; we come to expect these losses. These expectations, perhaps, are what make the unexpected or the accidental deaths of the young mother or the middle-aged bread-winner so tragic. These same expectations evoke trauma when a young child or teenager dies.

The trauma and tragedy of the deaths of most young people is felt and shared by many people — family, friends, neighbors, schoolmates, and the community. But what about the death of an infant? What are the reactions of parents, family, and community to the loss of infants? Who is the infant anyway? What is his or her identity? Is this a person to be mourned? There are certainly no wide circles of acquaintances. There are no classmates; there are no friends; there are no community contacts. There are only the mother, the father and, perhaps, the grandparents who really "know" the child. Therefore, can the loss of such an individual be so great? So significant? For these family members it certainly can be! For them, the infant is significant and the loss is real.

And what about the death of a fetus? Can this be such a great loss? For the mother, certainly, the loss is real; it has profound effects on her emotional, psychological, social, and even physical well-being for years. A period of grief and mourning, doubts and fears, questions with no answers, and intense sadness often follows fetal death. This period of grief is one that few people, beyond the immediate family, can really understand or comprehend. Most assuredly for the mother, and often for the father, these losses result in confusion, anger, bitterness, resentment, guilt, and a sense of failure. It is a time of intense loneliness and agonizing despair; it is also a time of reexamination and sometimes rejection of ingrained religious beliefs.

This heightened response to infant loss may stem from the fact that the death of an infant is usually unanticipated. It often comes quickly, without warning, after many months of active positive planning for the baby's arrival. As such, the loss is particularly disruptive. In some cases the loss may be the first child; in most cases the family itself is in the early, formative years; thus, the death of the infant may actually place the family in jeopardy by hindering or halting its further development. Family plans are disrupted; hopes for future growth are extinguished.

Though many fathers experience grief, the mother generally feels the impact of the loss more intensely. The lesser impact on the father does not imply that his reactions are insignificant. In most instances the paternal response to infant death is highly specific and individualized; maternal reactions, on the other hand, exhibit a great deal of similarity. Regardless of the type of loss, there appears to be a characteristic pattern of grief experienced by most mothers.

Nothing compares with, or surpasses, the anguish of the grieving mother. The intensity of her anguish is understandable when viewed in terms of the emotional attachment between mother and child that develops in the early months of pregnancy. Fetal/infant death, which results in an abrupt severing of this bond, produces a clearly defined and prolonged effect on the mother.

*Grieving
Mothers*

My husband and I feel quite lucky that we were able to get to know Stephen. He was born in a hospital with an excellent intensive care nursery and neonatal staff . . . . Both of us could remain with our son as much as we wanted. We could touch and fondle him and even share experiences with other parents. However, all the sympathy in the world could not console us when they told us he was dying . . . . Now, over a year later, it still hurts and we still cry; we are still angry. Even though we've thrown ourselves into a myriad of new activities to keep busy and physically fit, we really don't want to do anything. What we want is our son. What we want is for our hearts to be at peace and to end the torment and anguish.

These vivid words from a young legal secretary reflect the feelings and experiences of so many parents who have suffered the pain of losing an infant. Their grief is overpowering, and there appears to be neither escape nor relief. No matter what the parent, particularly the mother, feels or experiences prior to the loss, no matter what degree of planning or anticipation is involved, the death of a newborn, a young infant, or the loss of a viable fetus usually triggers intense grieving that will dominate her existence for days, weeks, months, even years.

Through both interviews and letters, many women have expressed to us their individual experiences with fetal or infant death. As we reviewed each case, certain similarities began to emerge that we believe to be quite common to the grieving mother. Before examining these similarities in detail, we want to summarize them.

COMMON CHARACTERISTICS OF GRIEVING MOTHERS

In the first place, all the mothers mourned, regardless of the kind of loss they experienced. We initially believed that a mother would be more emotionally distant from her child if she had miscarried at six months than if she had delivered a baby who lived for several hours or days before dying. Therefore we expected that grief expression would be less intense in cases of miscarriage than in stillbirth or neonatal death. This proved to be only partially true. Different grief expressions relating to the type of loss were apparent. Emotional distance also seemed to be important, but its importance was found only in the length of the mourning period. Little difference existed between the conception of the reality and the pain of the loss at the time the loss occurred. In other words, the duration of grieving was generally shorter in the case of fetal loss, but the initial expression of grief was just as intense. All mothers experienced some degree of grief.

Depending upon the type of loss — miscarriage, stillbirth, or neonatal death — specific emotions varied. Feelings of anger and bitterness were the more common expressions of mothers who lost children after birth (neonatal death) than of those who miscarried. However, feelings of guilt and of failure as a woman were often more intense for those who miscarried or delivered stillborn babies. The extreme guilt found among miscarriage and stillbirth mothers support the view that these women often conjure up images about what they did or didn't do during their pregnancies that caused them to abort or deliver a dead infant. These images include such things as wondering about their sexual activity, or the vitamins they may have conveniently forgotten to take, or the trip they did take, or the tennis match they played, or even the innocent action of climbing stairs. Regardless of the cause, the loss represented a traumatic and painful ordeal for each mother. In many cases this ordeal persisted for many years.

The second point is that the mothers vividly remembered details of the events surrounding the loss. Each mother was able to recall the specific circumstances of her pregnancy and loss. Even those who had lost an infant more than ten years earlier were able to recall the smallest details of the event. While studies have shown that the accuracy of details may be distorted somewhat, as a result of sedation, stress, or the passage of time, many of the details reported to us were perceived by the mothers to be accurate. These episodes had such an impact on these women's lives that they could remember all the sadness, sorrow, guilt, helplessness, and anger with precision, clarity, and emotion. They could, at any moment, vividly recreate specifics such as the things people said at the time, their physical surroundings, perhaps seeing and holding the baby, and the intense emotional outpouring they experienced at the time of their loss. This acute remembrance was one thing that all the mothers had in common without exception.

Third, the grieving mothers found communication channels closed to them. Professionals, family, and friends either avoided or discouraged discussion of the loss, and they often excluded the mother from many of the important decisions that were made. In many cases, even the husband became elusive as the mother desperately searched for receptive listeners. The women often found communication channels closed at precisely those times when the need was greatest for them to remain open. Family, friends, and others often created the impression that it was best for the mothers to forget the incident. This may have been the result of a well-intentioned protective attitude on their part, or their inability to recognize the significance of the loss, or their own uncomfortable feelings about death. Whatever the cause, the imposition of a cruel form of isolation, tending to amplify the emotional feelings and extend the mother's grief over a long period of time, resulted.

During the course of our interviews, we saw a great outpouring of emotion. Tears and crying were quite common as the mothers relived their experiences. In many cases these reactions came as a total surprise to the mothers, who, although aware of the nature of the interview beforehand, nevertheless did not anticipate the reactions they subsequently experienced. While we were initially disturbed by this outpouring of emotion and felt somewhat guilty that we were reopening old wounds, we soon realized that the interview sessions themselves were serving as therapy. In many cases we learned that the interview was the first opportunity that some mothers had had to express openly their feelings about the loss. They described the interview as "cleansing," "rewarding," "needed."

Fourth, husband-wife relationships often became strained. This unfortunate situation is the result of a breakdown in communications, a breakdown that stems from the different ways husbands and wives perceive their circumstances. From one point of view, owing to the different response patterns of husbands and wives, the wife may come to feel that her husband is not grieving and that he doesn't understand the depth of her feelings. This, in fact, may be true, particularly in the case of an early miscarriage, before the husband has established affectional ties with the infant. In this case the wife would experience more severe grief than the husband, who would prefer simply to put the whole experience behind them. This is hardly ever the case, however, in neonatal death, where the husband has had the opportunity to establish an emotional attachment with the infant. In this situation the couple's problems are compounded and stem, in part, from the husband's perception of his own grief in relation to his wife's. In these cases husbands grieve intensely, yet they feel they must be strong and supportive of their wives. Friends and relatives, who have the same expectations concerning the role of the husband, also share this attitude. Consequently, few people respond to the husband in an understanding way. They seldom realize that he, too, needs support and sympathy. The result is that husbands often become angry and resentful; they feel they are being left out or overlooked by those expressing sympathy to the mother. In either case, the situation severely assaults the stability of the marriage. It disrupts intimate relationships and often leads to a breakdown in sexual response and activity. This breakdown, in turn, can result in marital failure.

A fifth point was the unsatisfactory relationship many women had with their physicians. Apparently, few physicians (obstetricians and pediatricians, as well as family physicians) expressed much concern about the tragedy that struck these families. Those who did attempt to fill the role of counselor-consoler often said all the wrong things. Such expressions as "forget about this child," or "you are still young enough to have another," or "you should be glad that the baby was normally developed," or "you now have a little angel in heaven" are all examples of clichés that parents absolutely did not need or want to hear upon learning that their infant had died.

This apparent insensitivity of doctors may be due, in part, to the fact that their formal medical curriculum teaches them life-sustaining values, with little mention of death. Doctors react with attitudes that are oriented toward the living; consequently, these attitudes greatly hamper their effectiveness in dealing with death.

Certainly not all mothers and fathers had difficult relationships with their physicians. Some physicians were more progressive than others and recognized that the need for counseling and consoling often extends for weeks or months after the loss.

Six, unyielding hospital staff and inflexible hospital rules often hindered the resolution of grief. This is an area that can be improved greatly by simply (1) training hospital staff to deal more effectively with death, particularly infant death; and (2) training the staff to relate to their patients with more understanding and sensitivity. Nurses, ward attendants, and other support personnel often can create tremendous feelings of resentment, bitterness, and guilt by the ignorant and cold remarks they make to parents who have suffered losses and who need understanding and sympathy.

In response to inflexible rules, hospitals often treated women suffering losses in a rather unconcerned manner. For instance, they returned them to the obstetrical wards, where they could hear infants crying and see other mothers nursing, as if nothing had happened. We also found that mothers were seldom informed of their alternatives relative to seeing, holding, and taking pictures of their viable or nonviable infants. Lack of these opportunities may have led to an intensification of guilt, resentment, and even hostility.

Finally, the total resolution of maternal grief may never occur. Numerous mothers were still depressed a year after their loss. Some were still preoccupied with thoughts of the infant. The majority of women we studied also sensed that they would carry the burden of their losses throughout their lives. The emotions, feelings, and thoughts surrounding their losses had persisted, in milder form, for many years.

This finding of an extended period of grieving does not imply that grief continues to dominate one's existence, but, rather, that the experience of infant death and the attendant feelings do remain, ever so subtly, and are never entirely forgotten. "Shadow grief," as we have come to call it, is a different kind of grief, a less debilitating variety than that manifested in the early days or weeks following the loss. The difference between chronic grief and shadow grief is similar to a comparison of pneumonia and the common cold. The latter is less serious and more of a nuisance than anything else. Responses from women we interviewed graphically illustrate what we mean:

> It's been eight years for me and I still feel the hurt when I see a pregnant friend or hear a new baby cry.

> Although it has been twenty years since I lost my baby (stillbirth) at times I contemplate that night and still feel the sorrow.

> I think about her every year on her birthday and I pray to God that He has her in heaven with Him, so someday I can see her . . . Oh, how I long to see her.

> It's been nine years and I know I'll never really get over it . . . I'll never

get over it.

No one ever gets over that kind of anguish. It's been eleven years and I can still remember every detail and if I let myself, I can still feel all the hurt.

Subsequent chapters will elaborate on many of these findings. Some of the findings are based on empirical measurements and documentation that we can verify; others represent subjective conclusions drawn as a result of detailed study of our interview transcripts. Both the documented findings and the subjective conclusions are important for those professionals who work with grief-stricken mothers as well as for those loved ones — family and friends — who deal with them on a personal basis. They are also important for the mother herself; for she can come to realize that her deep-seated feelings and reactions are in no way abnormal or dissimilar to what other mothers experiencing many of the same problems have felt.

A LONELY GRIEF

What is this powerful phenomenon called grief and how is it expressed? For the purposes of this study, we define grief as a highly variable emotional, psychological, physical, and social response to the loss of a loved one through death. It has a known origin; in this case, it is the death of a baby. Grief may be openly expressed through behavior, such as weeping, screaming, hostility, and so forth; or it may remain hidden and unexpressed in feelings of guilt, bitterness, and sadness. The overt expression of grief can be highly beneficial to the person who has experienced a loss, for such an expression may serve to release pent-up emotions. Hidden grief, on the other hand, may remain unresolved; furthermore, it can be detrimental to the physical, mental, and social well-being of the grieving individual.

Two factors contribute to the intensity and the unusual nature of the grief reactions of mothers and fathers over the loss of their infants: (1) the suddenness and unexpected nature of the loss; and (2) the way infant death is socially defined in our culture.

Regarding the suddenness of the loss, the deaths usually occur without warning; they give the parents little time for preparation. For no apparent reason a "textbook" pregnancy may end in the birth of a stillborn child. Such an event may overwhelm the parents and shatter months of planning and preparation; or, the baby may be born prematurely, again with little warning. Premature babies are highly vulnerable to a wide range of disorders. In many cases, unless immediate action is taken, action usually involving the use of special equipment and skilled technology (most certainly in the case of early premies), death will follow in a matter of minutes or, at most, hours. In these cases, parents usually have an opportunity to prepare themselves, but that time is short. In other cases, miscarriage will occur in the fourth or fifth month of pregnancy. These, too, usually occur without warning in a rapid sequence of events. Full-term babies born with respiratory and other functional disorders, or those born as a result of birth trauma, will succumb, sometimes very quickly. These unanticipated developments leave the parents little time to prepare. Sudden Infant Death Syndrome, by definition, is also unexpected. In all of these cases intense grief emerges. Parents respond with shock, bewilderment, fear, anger, frustration, and guilt.

The unusual character of the grief at the loss of an infant is also determined by the second factor mentioned above: the way infant death is defined and perceived in our culture. The community — friends, neighbors, and even relatives — neither perceives, nor responds to, infant death in the same way as it does to the deaths of older, loved persons. The community tends to disregard the infant as a real, living person, and thus to disassociate "normal grief" in response to the loss of an older person from "pseudo grief" in response to infant loss. The death of an infant is less a "tragic" occurrence for the family and more an "unfortunate" one. Consequently, the community expects the mother's reaction to this "unfortunate" event to be short-lived and temporary.

The combination of these two factors, the suddenness of the loss and the lack of community responsiveness, creates a situation in which maternal grief is often expressed in a covert fashion. This maternal grief remains essentially unresolved, in some cases, for years. Most persons who have never actually experienced the loss of an infant do not understand the depth and intensity of the grief felt, nor can they comprehend the devastating impact that such losses have on the family organization.

As a consequence of the sudden loss and the lack of supportive response, the mother finds herself in an extremely difficult situation. She suffers intense grief, and she does so in virtual isolation. Even her husband cannot always comprehend the depth of her feelings, particularly in the case of a miscarriage. Her parents and other relatives, her friends and acquaintances, and in some cases even her physician, all respond with limited and short-lived compassion. In fact, the usual sympathies that are extended to individuals who lose a spouse, a parent, or an older child are generally not offered to parents who have lost an infant, particularly if the loss occurred in the prenatal period before the child was viable and observable. The feelings on the part of others seem to be that since the child was unknown, its death cannot be tragic. Therefore they encourage the grieving mother to "Get well! You can have others!"

What people do not realize is that this infant has been a part of the mother since its conception. She has come to know it in a way that no one else has. In a sense, she has lost not only a child but also a part of herself. Her breasts ache to nurse and her arms long to hold her lost infant. She feels empty, weak, and insecure; a very real and significant part of her has died. Maternal love, whatever its source, reaches deeply into the very earliest stages of pregnancy and attaches itself firmly to the growing infant. Loss of that infant is a very real experience and the mother's grief over that loss can become oppressive.

These generalizations obviously apply only to those mothers who want a child. It is interesting to speculate about the feelings of mothers who consciously make the decision to terminate an unwanted pregnancy. This would seem to be a difficult decision, even for those who experience few moral or religious objections. Our experience was that even those mothers who initially did not want the baby, whose pregnancies were unplanned, experienced a rather strong sense of love and attachment as the child developed. Upon their infant's death, they experienced an exceptionally strong sense of guilt stemming from their earlier feelings of rejection. For these mothers and fathers anguish and despair were often intensified.

Although fathers may experience a sense of loss in cases of miscarriage or stillbirth, their grief, in most cases, cannot really compare to that of the mother. While the husband tries to be supportive, there are many occasions when the wife believes her husband does not really understand the depth of her feelings. She is usually right. Many times this becomes a source of conflict within the family and leads to a breakdown in communication and an intensification of the mother's isolation. Thus many women experience a compounded feeling of loneliness, imposed not only by friends and relatives who prefer not to talk about the loss, but also by a husband who feels that talking about the baby only serves to keep the memories alive and prolong the wife's intense hurt, a hurt that he does not thoroughly understand anyway.

Thus the mother most often carries the burden of grief alone, without adequate avenues of expression. Sometimes this imposed isolation leads to a grief reaction that borders on the pathological. Pathological grief is characterized by a set of morbid reactions, which includes delusions, phobias, obsessions, and, in some cases, hallucinations. Although true pathological grief is probably not typical, there are cases in which it is difficult to distinguish it from a normal grief reaction.

Helen, for example, was a young mother whose infant girl died three days after birth as a result of birth trauma. During her interview, she revealed certain aspects of her behavior that she had never discussed with anyone else, including her husband. She also noted that the interview was the first opportunity she had had in ten years to discuss her loss. She now recognizes that her reaction at the time was partially prompted by an inability to discuss the irrational nature of her feelings and subsequent behavior with her husband, whom she believed had no interest in her feelings and did not understand.

Below is an excerpt from her interview in which she describes her rather unusual behavior. The reader can judge whether it should be considered pathological or not:

She was buried in a little place just for babies and every time I would go to visit her, there would be more babies. I felt she had lots of company and was not alone. I worried about her getting cold and all sorts of things. I remember one day in particular I was sitting by the grave and I thought, maybe I could dig it up; it wasn't very deep. I was really serious. I don't know what I would have done with her if I would have dug it up but I can vividly remember having this thought. I think I felt guilty about not seeing her one last time at the funeral home and not holding her. I remember I would talk to her and tell her how sorry I was for not seeing her and not holding her. I worried about the cold and the bugs getting to her body — that bothered me a lot! I went to her grave three or four times a week over a period of three or four months. I could not help myself; something was pulling me there . . . . [And] while kneeling there, it would take all my energy to keep from tearing at the earth. There was absolutely no one I could talk to about all these strange feelings I was experiencing; not even my husband; he just kept telling me that she was not really there, that she was in heaven, but I guess I couldn't accept this. Then one day I found myself sitting at the grave with a popsicle stick in my hand scratching and pulling at the dirt and suddenly I realized what I was doing. I was, in fact, digging for that little coffin!

Fortunately, Helen was able to recognize the irrationality of her behavior and pull herself back from the brink. Others are not so fortunate. They find themselves in need of psychiatric care.

THE STAGES OF GRIEF

Grief reactions vary in type and intensity. Most of them can be grouped under one of three general categories: (1) emotional and/or psychological effects; (2) physical effects; and (3) social effects. Emotional and psychological reactions include denial, guilt, anger, resentment, bitterness, depression, time confusion, irritability, sadness, sense of failure, concentration problems, failure to accept reality, and preoccupation with thoughts and memories of the deceased. Common physical effects include exhaustion, loss of appetite, sleeping problems, lack of strength, weight loss, headache, blurred vision, breathlessness, and palpitations. Social effects generally include withdrawal from participation in normal activity, and isolation, which may include an emotional, and sometimes physical, separation from a spouse. In serious cases grief can also manifest itself in various forms of pathological emotional disorders and physical distress.

As individuals grieve, they pass through a series of stages, each characterized by identifiable emotions and specific reactions such as those mentioned above. Robert Kavanaugh, in *Facing Death* (Penguin, 1974), discusses seven stages of the grieving process. He states that, "Within each of the seven [stages], we can notice typical feelings, distinct reactions to these feelings and definite needs or cries for help." The seven stages are (1) shock, (2) disorganization, (3) volatile emotions, (4) guilt, (5) loss and loneliness, (6) relief, and (7) reestablishment.

These stages are distinct, yet they interconnect and overlap.

They need not occur in sequence or in any particular time frame. Some stages can be passed over entirely; others may last for only a short period of time; and still others may continue for long periods. Setbacks and reversals are common. Certain stages may repeat themselves months or years later as a result of any number of causes and unique circumstances. We believe that those people who have contact with the grieving mother should understand this staging process as it pertains to her.

A step-by-step analysis of the seven stages of grief, which focuses upon the reactions of those mothers we interviewed, will highlight characteristic responses as well as problems that arose for them.

Shock

Without a doubt, shock is the most common initial reaction when the attending physician first tells a mother that her baby did not survive or is very close to death. Since she had expected a normal delivery and a healthy child, the shock is severe and is usually accompanied by disbelief and denial. "It can't be true;" "This is not really happening to us" are common responses. Shock is a normal reaction, a self-protective device. It is a defense against the overwhelming feelings of loss.

The shock plunges the mother into an unreal world, a fantasy where her dreams and plans for the future turn rapidly into a nightmare. Mothers compare this stage with that of a horrible dream from which they feel they will shortly awaken with a healthy child. This is an understandable reaction, especially when we consider the influence of sedating drugs. One mother stated, "It's like being hit in the middle of the forehead with a hammer. You're absolutely stunned! Your legs turn to jelly. You can't — you won't — believe the words you're hearing."

Mothers in this stage often develop an emotional numbness

that is difficult to penetrate. They stare unemotionally; they mumble incoherently; they hear virtually nothing. Some scream and become hysterical; others become emotionally paralyzed, fixated somewhere between the world of fantasy and the world of reality. Janet, the mother of a six-month-old girl who died from an undetected birth defect, describes her reaction:

> We absolutely refused to believe it was anything serious. We held on to this belief all through the resuscitation efforts by the paramedic squad at home, during the trip to the hospital, and during the long wait in the emergency room. Both my husband and I refused to consider the fact that the situation was even serious, let alone fatal. When the doctor finally came in with tears in his eyes and told us Suzy was dead, we just sat there and literally could not comprehend what he was telling us. It was as though we were frozen in time. It must have been ten minutes before the horrible reality of it all hit us.

Even now, Janet cannot recall the precise feelings she experienced during those first few minutes after hearing that her daughter had died. For her, it was as if the world had suddenly stopped.

Martha, whose week-old child died on the operating table as doctors tried to correct a heart defect, illustrates another common shock reaction:

> I remember the doctor stood in the doorway when he told me. I had had a slight infection and was still in the hospital. He said — I'll never forget his words — "Ginger did not survive the operation . . . ." When he said those words, it just stunned me, like a blow. I guess I expected it but I really wasn't ready for those words — I don't think anyone ever is. All I did was stare at him for what apparently was a long period of time. And then, rather matter-of-factly, I started to thank him for all he had done when all of a sudden it hit me, that everything was over, that there was nothing more that could be done! I then became hysterical and remember very little from that point on. It was several hours before I was able to get control of myself.

Those people who are in a position to comfort mothers as they pass through this stage of shock must realize that little can be done until the initial shock subsides. Just being there, offering physical and emotional support by one's mere presence, is an important contribution.

Usually, the stage of shock is short-lived. It may last for minutes, or at most, hours. In a few exceptional cases, however, it might extend for months, overlapping other stages, and becoming the dominant characteristic of the entire grief response. This happened to Sandra, the mother of a seven-month-old victim of SIDS. She recalls:

> It was one year, almost to the day, after Billy's death before I truly became aware of what had really happened to us. I maintained myself on tranquilizers for one year, living in what I now believe to be a constant state of shock and denial.

There is really no way that a mother can deal personally with such shock. By the time she becomes aware of it, it has subsided. In fact, the bereavement process itself, characterized by an outpouring of grief, does not begin until the shock has abated and the individual has progressed to the next stage.

Disorganization

During the stage of shock and emotional numbness, few other reactions will be apparent. When parents begin to respond in other ways, when they actually begin to mourn, shock begins to subside. They then begin to move into the second stage — disorganization.

In this stage confusion abounds. Parents will still experience anguish, sadness, and crying; but the central feature is disorganization and confusion. "What do we do now?" "How do we handle this?" "Who do we call?" "What do we say?" Their circumstances and surroundings become totally out of focus. This is a crippling time for most parents — a time for touching, holding, caressing, hugging — for physical contact — a time for crying. It is a time for talking. They talk, talk, talk, without interruption, without logic, without any sense being made of what they are saying. Fortunately, simply talking and expressing their feelings and moods has a therapeutic value at this point. It also helps to dissipate their overwhelming sadness and physical anguish.

This definitely is not the time, however, for making important decisions or for dealing with important information. Parents are seldom able to recall events that happened during this period. Therefore all important decisions about the future, about the funeral and burial, about the cause of death and autopsy results, should be postponed, if possible, until the disorganization and general confusion of this phase has begun to fade. Sometimes, however, important decisions cannot be postponed. When this is the case, those presenting the options to the parents should respect their state of mind; otherwise the parents may, at a later time, regret their decisions. Margaret, whose infant was stillborn, summed it up adequately:

> We were so confused. We didn't know whether we were coming or going. We had all those decisions to make — about the funeral and whether or not to name the baby, and where to bury it and everything. I just agreed to everything that was suggested and now I really resent it. I have very bitter feelings, particularly about the funeral and how the burial arrangements were handled. I know it was partly our fault but they should have known that we were in no condition to make rational decisions at that time.

Margaret is referring to members of the hospital staff who prompted her husband to select a "package" arrangement for the burial of their son with no service or funeral, and the funeral director, who required that the parents make a decision on the basis of one type of procedure, giving them no alternatives to consider. Usually this occurs under the guise of being the "usual way these things are handled."

Both mothers and fathers need a great deal of support during this time of disorganization. They need to express their deepest fears and anxieties and to receive reassurances from those around them. They need to discuss their feelings, not only with their doctors and other members of the hospital staff, but also with each other. They need to unleash their feelings and cry and grieve together. Often, however, this mutual sharing does not take place. The husband may feel he must hide his true feelings. He may turn away from his wife to "protect" her from the anguish of his own grief, or he may simply be too personally stricken to offer her the support she needs. Whatever the reason, the husband eventually feels that he must overcome his feelings to hold the family together. Consequently, the period of disorganization may be much shorter-lived for the husband than for his wife, who may remain in a state of confusion for a longer time, much to his dismay. Sometimes, the mother will even feel that she must be strong for the sake of her husband and other people. These attitudes only serve to suppress other feelings and extend the period of disorganization. This combination of events can be observed in Barbara's reaction to her husband's response after the stillbirth of their infant:

> I really don't believe Tom fully understood what I was going through. I was terribly confused and upset. I needed to talk through some things and resolve some of these feelings, but he simply refused to talk about the baby. I guess he felt it would be too upsetting for me. God, how I wanted to talk! But he just never would and I guess I resented it, deeply. . . . I cried incessantly, for weeks on end, and it started to affect our relationship. I realized it had to stop, and I developed an unusual existence. I would wander from room to room during the day, completely debilitated — crying. But at five o'clock, I would shut it off until the next day. Finally, I returned to work and the crying stopped, but those initial weeks without support from my husband were disorganized, confusing, and difficult.

Volatile Emotions

As confusion and disorganization subside and the mother's mind begins to clear, the reality of the loss begins to return. As this happens, emotions erupt. Frequently, emotional outbursts take the form of displaced anger or rage. This appears to be a common response of fathers, especially those who use anger or rage as a substitute for other more debilitating and less "masculine" forms of grief.

Anger and hostility can appear suddenly, sometimes within minutes of hearing the news. Some fathers become very physical and attack and try to destroy whatever is close by. One young father, recovering rather quickly from the shock of hearing of his son's death, flew into a rage and plunged his fist through the wall of the emergency room. Obscenities and invectives may be shouted for everyone to hear, sometimes directed at the doctor and hospital staff, sometimes at ambulance attendants and paramedic squads, and sometimes even at the spouse. God quite often becomes a target of vindictive outbursts and angry gestures, too.

Angry parents are difficult to deal with and relate to. No one likes to be around hostility, jealousy, resentment, and vindictiveness. Friends and relatives of grieving parents, therefore, need to recognize this stage and to offer compassion and understanding, not criticisms, harsh judgments, and admonishments.

No one can predict how long this phase of volatile emotions will last. Sometimes it is only momentary. The parent will lash out and the episode will be quickly forgotten. In other cases, it will be longer lasting. The parent will slowly regain control and composure. Each of us has a different way of handling hostility when it surfaces.

Some parents try not to let their anger show in public. Instead, they lash out in the privacy of their homes, where they often direct their hostility toward family members. Others cannot contain themselves and engage in explosive behavior, which is often condemned by those around them. This condemnation only intensifies their hurt and despair. We should remember that anger and hostility are reflections of more basic feelings of helplessness and frustration that can be vented only through volatile outbursts.

Thomas, a father whose child of four months died unexpectedly from genetic complications, described his experience:

> My anger was difficult to control. I was so depressed that I often responded with hostility. I can't really explain that feeling . . . . It was as if every little thing irritated me to the point of overt anger. I was an absolute brute with my wife. I remember this feeling lasted for several days.

George, a father whose daughter died of a respiratory disease one week after birth, recalls his feelings as he accompanied her to a neonatal unit in another hospital:

> I remember I was so angry that this was happening to us. Here my wife was lying in another hospital and I was there, standing around helplessly, not knowing whether my daughter was alive or dead. Then, when she died, I thought, "Christ! What a waste!" All I could do was pound my fist on the table . . . . I don't think I had a civil word to say to anyone. It was two or three weeks before I was finally able to let go and get it all out.

In a sense, screaming and hysterics, reactions more common among mothers, can also be defined as a symptom of this stage of volatile emotions. Such behavior often occurs during the stage of shock. When postponed, however, it may take on the character of an angry outburst. A young mother, who knowingly carried a dead baby for two weeks, described her violent reaction, which did not occur until several days after delivery.

> I was in a state of shock for the two weeks I carried him. I couldn't cry — I tried — but I just couldn't. I couldn't feel . . . . I know it sounds

weird. My husband would not come near me during that time. I guess he was repulsed or something . . . . But, I remember, it must have been a week or so after it was over. I thought I was getting along fine and then one day I was sitting at the breakfast table and WHAM! . . . it hit me — I had lost our child! I just screamed and screamed. My husband came running in and tried to console me but nothing helped. I became like a wild person . . . he had to hold me to keep me from hurting myself. If anyone had seen me then, they would have thought I was a basket case for sure.

Mary tells of another kind of emotional hostility. She directed it toward her infant and herself. She, too, had carried a dead baby, for eight days prior to delivery.

I would walk through the house from room to room cussing and swearing at that baby. I would pound my stomach with my fists until I was literally "black and blue." That baby was a part of me and now it was dead and I guess I blamed and hated myself for allowing it to happen.

Guilt

As anger and hostility begin to subside, the mother, often exhausted and overwrought, will collapse into the fourth stage, guilt. Almost all mothers experience this phase of the grieving process. Guilt usually comes in waves. At times, it penetrates the very core of the mother's existence. Parents who have experienced SIDS, for example, find that guilt is an overpowering and dominant feature of the entire grieving process. In other types of loss it may be more subtle, but it remains, nevertheless, very real. "I should not have taken that trip;" "I should not have done those exercises;" "I should not have taken those pills."

Parents, particularly mothers, often feel that they are to blame for the loss. The mother commonly searches her behavior patterns prior to the death of the infant for clues that will give her the logical reason for its occurrence. In cases of stillbirths and miscarriages, mothers will think back over their behavior prior to the loss and admonish themselves for not recognizing what have since become tell-tale signs of trouble — aches, cramps, spotting, or minor bleeding. Often they feel that if they had taken better care of themselves, if they had taken those vitamins, if they had followed that diet, the loss would not have occurred. They wonder about the influence of sexual activity, strenuous exercise, climbing stairs; they even wonder if their thoughts could have influenced the outcome. In the case of neonatal death, other, similar self-admonishments occur.

Louise relates what amounts to pathological guilt stemming from her thoughts after the birth of her son:

> My husband left me when I was seven months pregnant. All I had heard up to that time was, "I can't wait to have a son," "Wonder what my boy will look like," etc. After he left the only thing I could think about was having a daughter. I wanted a girl so badly. You guessed it! I had a boy. I know I was wrong, but I continued even after his birth to wish he was a girl . . . . I really flew into a rage when my mother-in-law said, "He looks like his father." My only thought was "I don't want this boy!" He died about two weeks later and I knew I had killed him . . . . It took eighteen months of psychiatric care to overcome the guilt.

Sometimes the wife or husband directs the blame outward toward the other. If there were infants on the husband's side of the family who had died in the past, the wife may hold him to blame. In other cases, the husband will blame his wife for her "neglect" of herself or for not being conscious enough to recognize early signs of trouble. Many times these feelings are not openly expressed but rather lie fermenting below the surface, erupting at a later time. With some couples they persist and lead to stresses and strains in family relationships. Ann, who miscarried at three months told us:

> I sometimes get the feeling even today that my husband held me

responsible for what happened. I was playing tennis the day the cramps started and when I told him about it (the tennis) later he hit the roof. He has never said anything but I get the feeling that that's how he feels. Maybe someday we will be able to talk about it, I don't know.

Judy, who miscarried at five months, indicated that although her husband was supportive, other relatives found ways to attach blame. She said:

My sister-in-law was so adamantly opposed to my working during my pregnancy that I believe she really felt that had I not been working, I would not have miscarried. She hurt me badly. She told me that if I had really wanted that child I would have quit working. She was the only one who made me feel that I was responsible. It took me a long time to get over that feeling of accusation.

All the questions begin to bubble to the surface during the guilt phase. The big question is always, Why? For the vast majority of mothers and fathers, the loss they suffer is basically unintelligible from the standpoint of moral or ethical reasons. In fact, this is often true for any loss during the early years of life. The expectation we hold for the young is life — not death. Therefore, the deaths of babies are "unexpected," "unplanned," "accidental," "senseless," and "useless," regardless of the medical reason. Therefore, medical reasons or causes of death are important information and should be shared with the parents as soon as such information becomes available. Autopsy results explained in layman's language can do much to relieve the mother's guilt.

Irene, whose three-week-old infant died in her arms from a deformed main heart artery while she was sitting in her pediatrician's waiting room, said this about guilt:

Yes, I definitely suffered tremendous guilt. I really wondered . . . . It was my first child and I wondered if I did something wrong. Or should I have known there was something wrong. She wasn't eating much and maybe this should have been my clue. I kept thinking over and over maybe I should have known there was something wrong! It wasn't until I got the autopsy results that I knew there was nothing that I could have done.

Joan, whose baby lived for eighteen hours after birth, relates her feelings of guilt and self-blame:

My delivery was horrendous. It should have been Caesarian. Two months after I found out I was pregnant, I was in the delivery room. A six-month delivery is very rough. I was tied down and I literally became hysterical. I wasn't prepared for it, no one talked to me, no one at all. It seemed like they were doing everything for the baby and nothing for me. I was fighting the delivery all the way, making it difficult on the baby, not to mention the doctor and myself . . . . I realized that when I saw how beat up the baby was. He was really bruised. I felt just terrible . . . . After I saw that, all I could think about was how selfish I was . . . . And then when he died, Oh God, I suffered from that for months!

Another important emotional effect that appears during this phase is a sense of failure as a mother and as a woman. These feelings, along with guilt, appear almost universally among grieving mothers. This is understandable, given the emphasis our culture places on reproduction in marriage. For many women, becoming pregnant and producing a healthy child represents both the fulfillment of themselves as women and the consummation of their marriages as mothers. Laura, who miscarried at four months, tells of her feelings of failure:

When I did miscarry, the fear that something was wrong with me was tremendous . . . . "What if I'm not going to be able to have a healthy child? What if this is just going to keep happening over and over again?"

These feelings of failure often develop as a result of the situations surrounding the mother, of the way others respond to her, and, particularly, from the insensitive things others say to her. The mother's feelings of failure are an important consideration for those who have contact with her. Her self-concept has been badly damaged, and she is exceptionally vulnerable at this time in her life. We must "handle with care" and "proceed with caution." Certainly we should encourage discussion, but with sensitivity and consideration.

Linda, whose baby was anacephalic and survived only for a few minutes, revealed how her feelings of failure developed:

> I think I had definite feelings of failure as a woman; however, I don't really think I felt that way initially. It was only after my obstetrician told me in a rather abrupt manner that what happened to me did not mean that I was inadequate as a woman. He said this and then promptly disappeared. Well, the very fact that he articulated this caused me to adopt these feelings and they persisted for a very, very long period of time.

Brenda, whose three-day-old infant died of hyaline membrane disease, recalled that she really had no such feelings until she had a sad encounter with an insensitive brother-in-law:

> The cruel things that unthinking people will say to you can greatly affect your self-image. I will never forget, if I live to be a hundred, what my brother-in-law said to me. This was about six months after we lost the baby. My sister had recently delivered and we were at the christening party. My sister could not yet drive and I was kidding her, I said "Hey, according to my doctors, you get to drive two weeks after you have the baby." And my brother-in-law said "Brenda, it's a lot easier when you don't bring a baby home. Shirley's had a tough time and she has to take care of this baby." I was absolutely stunned. He said it in front of everybody. I was so hurt. I went out into the yard and cried. The next day I called my sister and apologized for crying at her child's christening and all she said was "Well I won't tell Bill," as if I were at fault and Bill did the right thing. That really increased my sense of failure and it took me a long time to get over it.

Feelings of failure are not only characteristic of wives and mothers; some husbands also experience them. Ron, for example, projected this attitude upon his feelings of failure as a son. His mother was elderly and he was an only child. Much of his identity was wrapped up in his perception of his ability to give his mother a grandchild. His wife miscarried on two separate occasions. His feelings of failure were expressed as follows:

> I'm an only child; my dad died twenty years ago. My mother always talked about grandchildren and I've always wanted to have one for her. I was really more upset about that because I thought "Here's my chance to pay her back for all those years she cared for me without my dad." I thought we blew it, you know.

The sense of failure and the accompanying guilt can extend beyond the inability of being a father or mother to the potential inability to fulfill other roles in life. Parents want children for many different reasons. Community and social pressures are important variables. Simply observing other pregnant mothers, perhaps friends and relatives, can produce a strong desire to become pregnant; friends, parents, and in-laws can exert nonverbal pressures. Under these circumstances feelings of failure and guilt may be more intense because the mother may feel she has not only failed herself but has also failed to meet the expectations of others. Marie stressed her intense desire to become pregnant and the encouragement she received.

> Oh I really wanted that baby . . . . you can't imagine how I wanted that baby! Everyone — my family, my friends — was so supportive and so happy for me. It was such a good feeling; it was the greatest thing that ever happaned. Then in the third week of my eighth month, they couldn't find a heartbeat and the baby was stillborn a week later. My God, you wouldn't believe what I went through, particularly, to have to face my family and friends.

Joanne's feelings were similar:

Two of my friends were pregnant at the same time and we just had a ball together, planning and talking. I guess I was so proud of the fact that I was pregnant. My husband was elated and my family overjoyed. This would have been the first grandchild for both my husband's and my parents . . . . They would call me practically every day to see how I was doing . . . . Then I started getting really big and I thought at the time they were twins. We were all absolutely overjoyed. Well, I found out it was all water . . . . I had hydramnios . . . . I delivered prematurely and the baby — a little girl — died two days later. Let me tell you, the grief I suffered was excruciating. It was hell! I thought I had let the whole world down.

Loss and Loneliness

As the mother begins the process of working through her feelings of guilt and failure, the sense of loss and loneliness begins its assault. This is probably the most difficult phase of the grieving process. The sense of loss and loneliness represents subtle feelings that settle upon her gradually, almost unnoticed at first, but which later become intolerable. The horrible emptiness that the mother feels as she sits at home day after day contemplating her loss is almost beyond description.

Chris, whose infant was stillborn, thinks back on her experience during this phase:

I grieved most of the time by myself, because everybody's attitude was: "Well, that happens every day, you'll have another! You'll get over it, honey!" They pat you on the shoulder and treat you more like you've just lost a pet. So, my grief was a very personal kind . . . quiet . . . . I didn't even feel like I could talk to my husband about a lot of it because I didn't think he was feeling like I was feeling. So, I would say that it was a very lonely kind of grief — the same feelings every day. You think you're going crazy because you can't get it off your mind. My God, everybody loses babies, and you can have another! Still you can't get it off your mind. After a while you begin to wonder if you're

not neurotic. I was feeling depressed for months without really realizing it until I began feeling better. When I look back, I think, "My God,
what a nightmare!"

The central psychological responses during this period are
depression and intense sadness. Depression may not be constant. It
usually alternates with periods of normalcy when the mother feels
that perhaps she can cope. Depression often occurs in the quiet of
one's bed at night, when friends and neighbors have departed, and
the hustle and bustle of the day has ended. It is usually during these
quiet times that the reality of the loss becomes most oppressive and
depression most debilitating. It is not unusual for alternating
feelings of depression and normalcy to recur for weeks, sometimes
months.

This stage of grief usually emerges after the mother has
returned home and the family has apparently returned to its normal
activity. During these times mothers say they yearn to embrace
their baby; their arms ache to hold the baby; their breasts ache to
nurse the baby.

During this phase mothers also experience a concentration of
intense, agonizing symptoms of grief. Sleeping problems and
insomnia are common, as are loss of appetite, preoccupation with
thoughts and memories of the baby, problems in concentrating and
keeping one's mind on the tasks of the moment, repetitive dreams
of the baby, exhaustion, lack of strength, and irritability. Many
feelings, thoughts, and emotions manifest themselves during this
phase. It is a time of grief that can last for many months after
family, friends, and the community consider support and consolation no longer necessary.

Many mothers experience great difficulty in their encounters
with babies and pregnant women. This reaction is quite common
through all phases of the grief process; during this phase of loss and
loneliness feelings of sadness often turn to feelings of jealousy,

resentment, and in some cases, bitterness where other babies and pregnant women are concerned. Relatives and friends often do not understand these feelings; consequently, they think the young mother is being childish when she turns away from young babies. One woman's difficulties were expressed in this way:

> It really bothered me to see other pregnant women who were successfully pregnant [and] about to have babies having showers . . . . [This] was very difficult because they represented what I felt I had failed at. I think I felt that way through the miscarriage, through the pregnancy that wasn't working out, [and] through the second pregnancy until I had gotten past three months. I had a lot of feelings like that . . . . I think I had definite feelings of jealousy.

Another remarked:

> I just couldn't have anything to do with other babies. I had strong feelings of bitterness toward anyone who got pregnant. My best friend found out she was pregnant shortly afterwards. I'm not sure if it was bitterness, envy, or what, I don't know. All I know is that it made me cry a lot when I found out she was pregnant . . . . This was probably the biggest blow. I wished her well, but down deep, I thought it should have been my turn.

Another woman's difficulties were manifested in this manner:

> I would actually walk across the street to avoid babies. We were living in an apartment at the time and it seemed like there were babies everywhere! I would not go out for several weeks because I had this horrible fear that I would meet someone with a small baby and I would have to say something nice. It was really bad.

A real problem encountered by almost everyone suffering a loss, but particularly in the case of the loss of a planned and anticipated infant, is that of entering the empty nursery. Returning home from the hospital can be a particularly painful ordeal for both the mother and the father. Generally, the family has been preparing for this child since the mother first discovered her pregnancy; baby clothes and baby furnishings have been purchased; the room has been prepared. All these preparations, plus the psychological readiness experienced by the parents, must now, in some way, be nullified. The husband or some other close relative usually undertakes the dismantling process prior to the mother's return home. In many cases it is not possible to remove all traces of the months of preparation. Clothes and diapers can be packed away, but furniture and the nursery itself cannot be completely hidden from view. Its mere presence often creates or contributes to a heightened sense of loss and loneliness. Daily associations with these remembrances can be painful indeed. Many times, mothers resent the acts of well-meaning relatives who remove evidence of the baby's presence by packing away artifacts and clothes and storing them in inaccessible places around the house. They spend hours searching for evidence of their baby. They often feel a need to look at the baby clothes, to touch them, and to know that the experience was indeed real and not some horrible nightmare. It is advisable that the mother always be consulted about the disposition of the baby's things prior to their disposal. For many the nursery and its contents have genuine therapeutic value. The therapy it affords helps the grieving mother come to terms with the loss and diminishes her subsequent feelings of loneliness. The responses of three mothers illustrate the therapeutic value of retaining some evidence of the preparations for the baby. Martha had this to say:

> Relatives often have good intentions but they can sure mess things up by doing things that they think will be of help to you. By the time I got home from the hospital all the baby things were put away because the family thought it was best. There was a feeling of hate and invasion in my mind because they had done something that belonged to my husband and me privately.

Cathy said:

> The baby's nursery was my sanctuary. I would sit sometimes for hours in that nursery just crying and thinking and remembering. Although it was painful, I think it helped me deal with it all.

Nancy expressed her feelings thus:

> By the time I got home, everything was put away and out of sight. I was greatly upset by this. My husband thought it was the right thing to do. I didn't tell him how much this bothered me, but I greatly resented it. The first week I was home I dug everything out again and put it all back in the nursery. I told my husband I wanted it that way because I just needed to remember.

Relief and Reestablishment

The final stages of the grieving process have many labels. Sometimes they are called "relief and reestablishment," and sometimes "reorganization," and sometimes "reconstitution." All of the labels, however, imply a resolution of the grief process, an ending, the stage when the guilt and the sense of loss and loneliness begin to soften.

This is the phase when reminders of the loss, such as the nursery and the baby's things, can be confronted without emotions bubbling to the surface. The misery and despair begin to fade. The self-doubt, the guilt, the anger, the bitterness, all begin their journey out of existence as the grieving process moves into the final phase. Appetite returns, sleeping problems are overcome, strength returns, irritability diminishes. Dreams and preoccupation with thoughts of the deceased infant become less frequent. Depression subsides. The mother can now face each day with renewed interest in people, events, and things. Kavanaugh, in *Facing Death*, gives a very poetic description of this phase:

> As hope and fantasy approach reality, verdant meadows lie ahead, blue skies over open roads, excitement and extended hands — all

promises of a new ability to walk alone. Fantasies fade into constructive efforts to reach out and build anew. The phone is always answered, the door as well, and meetings seem important, invitations are treasured and any social gathering becomes an opportunity. Concrete steps replace wild reveries. Momentos of the past are put away for occasional family gatherings. New clothes and new places promise dreams instead of only fears (p. 122).

For most women, relief comes with the birth of a subsequent child. For mothers who want children, having a healthy subsequent child goes a long way in resolving their grief for the previous loss. In fact, many mothers told us that it was only after another birth that they knew that they had "made it." Their lives could then be put back together.

The twin stages of relief and reestablishment find expression in all those things that make us truly human, loving, and caring. We become whole again and open our hearts and arms to those around us. We reestablish ourselves once more with the living and with the joys of life. It is a genuine feeling of relief to be able to shed the months of guilt and failure, anger and hostility, depression and anxiety. The women who have progressed through the stages discover that they can once again fondle babies, that they can encounter pregnant women without jealousy and resentment, that they can enter nurseries without experiencing the intense pain of previous months, and that they can have discussions of the loss without the worry that they may be "upsetting." For those who achieve this phase of recovery, the grieving process will gradually draw to a close.

SHADOW GRIEF

The final stage of reestablishment never arrives all at once. Unfortunately, for many mothers, the satisfaction that comes from resolving the grief and sadness never arrives at all. Mothers tell us that there is always "something" that remains, difficult to pinpoint exactly; but because of it, their lives will never be the same again.

We have discovered through our interviews that the grief that mothers experience may never be completely resolved. Portions of it will always remain tucked away, appearing from time to time when they least expect it. We believe that "shadow grief," as we call it, is that "something" these mothers speak of, a burden that most of them will bear for the rest of their lives.

Shadow grief does not manifest itself overtly; it does not debilitate the individual. No effort is required to cope with it. In fact, a fairly established normal existence is usually resumed. On the surface, most observers would say that the grief has been resolved and the individual has resumed a normal life.

How then is shadow grief experienced? For one thing, it has a tendency to pop up insidiously on special occasions, such as birthdays, or death days. It can occur at times when the mother is forced to recall her loss, such as during our interview sessions. Shadow grief reveals itself through the form of a dull, unresponsive ache or an emotional dullness in which the person is unable to respond fully and completely to outer stimulation. She can laugh and appear to enjoy life, but the dull ache in the background remains constant and, under certain circumstances, surfaces. Frequently, it's in the form of tears, but it is always accompanied by a mild feeling of sadness and, sometimes, even a sense of anxiety. Shadow grief can vary in intensity depending upon the person and the unique factors involved. It is more emotional for some than for others.

Mary, whose infant was stillborn eight years prior to her interview said:

His birthday is especially difficult for me, since it is also his death day. I can still cry if I let myself, particularly on that day. All the pain seems to come back. I guess nothing can be done about it. I just know it will be a bad day for me.

Another young mother who lost a seven-month-old twin from a liver disease related the following:

> All I heard was how lucky I was that I still had one fine healthy baby left . . . . I was so used to doing everything for two babies — bathing, dressing, feeding, and so on. Now I am doing all this for one. When I go to the baby's room, I can still remember having two cribs . . . . It has been four years and Michael is a constant reminder to me of Joseph, the one I lost. I love Michael dearly, but I also loved Joey . . . . Joey is gone, but his image is still with me . . . . I see him everyday in Michael and I know this is the way it will always be.

Edna also illustrates, in her short description, the remnants of shadow grief:

> Wednesday morning when we heard the date on the radio, I remarked to my son that it was his sister's birthday. [Their daughter died of pneumonia at the age of four weeks, sixteen years before.] And I will tell you that I may not weep uncontrollably anymore, but tears still well up in my eyes whenever I tell someone of Sandra.

Shadow grief is certainly not the exclusive property of women who have lost infants; it can and does appear in regard to other kinds of losses, such as the loss of an older child, a dearly loved spouse, or a parent. Regardless of the form it may take, it is a common characteristic of the postmourning response.

Retention of grief in this form is most likely the result of two related factors that probably do not operate in other types of losses. One of these factors is the desire of mothers never to forget their losses. These mothers want to remember all the details. As they remember, they experience a mild emotional reaction. Mothers have told us that they actually feel better when they are able to cry, because when they are crying, they are remembering. In fact, they often experience pangs of guilt when they laugh and feel happy, because at those times they feel they are not remembering.

The other factor that may account for the retention of shadow grief is the general inability of the mother to express feelings with the spouse or sympathetic listeners outside, but close to, the family. This factor is closely tied to their desire to remember, and may, in fact, serve as the source of this desire. Unable to find legitimate avenues of expression, the need to remember becomes paramount. The mothers believe that if they do not remember, no one else will; the memory of their child must be kept alive at all costs.

Mothers have told us that they became physically and emotionally isolated after the loss of their infants. Often, after the initial conference with their physician about the circumstances of the death, it seems to them that no one ever again mentions the child; it is as though the child has never existed, a situation they find intolerable.

Even if husbands and wives are able to communicate, they find that it is usually short-lived. They discover that grief cannot be shared for long. There is an old saying that "grief shared is grief diminished." We find this adage difficult to accept. An individual suffering from intense sorrow can be of no support to his or her mate. When people are pressed to their own limits to take care of their own needs, they cannot be expected to offer much in the way of support and reassurance to others.

Many parents fail to grasp the significance of this. Their feelings often turn to resentment and bitterness when they find they cannot really depend upon each other in their time of greatest anguish. Therefore, the time comes when both need listeners who are detached from the sorrow of the situation and can appreciate their feelings without passing judgment. Unfortunately, because of the unique characteristics of this type of loss, sympathetic listeners are difficult to find. Consequently, mothers feel that remembrances of their infants will be lost forever without outlets for discussion and expression. Their grief becomes bottled up and parts of it remain unresolved, seeping out in shadow form years afterward. Michael, a twenty-six-year-old father, comments on the communication problem experienced by so many grieving parents:

> We had one burning need through the first year after Billie's death and that was simply to talk to someone, anyone, about how we felt. However, wherever we looked, no one was willing to listen.

Linda, a thirty-year-old mother of a stillborn son tells us of her communication problem:

> If I just had someone to talk to . . . . My husband was somewhat indifferent . . . . All these things pile up in your mind. When you can't talk about him, you get the feeling you're losing him. I couldn't talk to my friends because they just didn't want to listen. You just need someone . . . . Everybody needs someone . . . . I needed someone.

One way of coping with shadow grief is to realize that it will likely be a continuing part of one's existence. It will always be there, irrespective of wishes or efforts to do away with it. Parents who have lost infants are special people in the sense that they have had an experience that few others can truly understand. Unfortunately, they must carry this burden. Many parents recognize this. They comprehend the impact that the loss has had on their lives and they adjust accordingly. They are able to live with the remnants of shadow grief quite successfully.

Can one ever be rid of shadow grief? In answer to this question, we must bear in mind that there is no substitute for extensive and intensive communication during the many phases of the grieving process. With an open, understanding, and empathetic reaction on the part of the larger community, and, particularly, among the smaller group of the family's more intimate associates, mothers may well come to deal effectively with all aspects of grief and escape shadow grief. It is up to others — friends, neighbors, and relatives of the grieving mother — to cultivate an atmosphere that will make this possible.

Personal Relationships

There were all these people. The worst thing I can remember is everyone telling me to "Perk up; it's all right; forget it; you can have another baby." But you see, it wasn't all right; I didn't want another baby, I wanted that one.

If I were to tell you all the pain and mental anguish I experienced when my baby died, it would take hours. Although it happened twenty-nine years ago, I have never forgotten the cruelty meted out to me under the guise of "Hospital Regulations." As a result, I never saw my daughter, but to this day I wish I had.

An expectant mother does not live in social isolation. From the moment she learns she is pregnant, both she and her pregnancy become the focus of attention of her husband, family, and friends. Day-to-day activities and discussion often revolve around "our expectant mother." When other topics for discussion are exhausted, it is easy to focus on the pregnancy. How are you feeling? Is it an active baby? Would you rather have a boy or a girl? What will you name it? For the people closest to her, as well as for the expectant mother herself, emotions develop from surprise to excitement to happy anticipation. Plans are made, fantasies abound, and active preparation for the new arrival begins.

For many women, the obstetrician becomes more than the doctor who gives them their necessary-but-unpleasant annual examination. The obstetrician now represents a very significant individual in their lives, and the visit they once dreaded becomes an eagerly awaited experience. Even in the larger clinics where an expectant mother may see a different physician on each visit, she still projects many positive emotions onto the doctor whose care she is in.

As the woman enters the hospital, the hospital staff becomes for her more than skilled and semiskilled functionaries. Throughout her stay she will have contact with the nurses, aides, and volunteers. While they, as people, are probably less important to the mother than her husband, family, friends, and physician, their contact and communications with her are equally significant, for they are the ones who will care for her throughout the hospital stay. The mother will search their communications, both verbal and nonverbal, for messages — from "everything is O.K." to "there might be a problem."

Close friends become cherished companions to share the happiness and anxieties of the pregnancy. Sometimes the expectant mother is comforted by one or two confidantes, who are either pregnant themselves or have recently had a child. Shopping for maternity clothes, having baby showers, and "sharing the pregnancy" are all important activities that extend through the entire period, from the initial announcement confirming the pregnancy to the climax of labor and delivery.

Grandparents and in-laws are usually intimately involved, and the birth of a grandchild, particularly the first, is a significant event in the lives of most grandparents-to-be. Not only do they feel a sense of pride in their children having children, but, having themselves produced a family in times of unsophisticated obstetric medicine, they also feel concern for the health of the mother and for the well-being of the unborn child. Both the pride and the concern are often communicated to the mother.

Of all those involved — physician, medical personnel, friends, and family — the husband is no doubt the most significant individual in the life of the expectant mother. From the cautious and sometimes secretive pregnancy test to the delivery itself, the husband is a focal point of both pride and concern. She feels pride in carrying the child that was created through their love for each other, sympathy for her husband's upcoming responsibility, and sometimes even concern about her appearance to him. She lets him share her pregnancy as much as possible; with the growing popularity of natural childbirth methods, he may indeed become involved in the total childbearing process. Whatever the circumstances, the mother constantly monitors the moods, expressions of feeling, and anxieties of her husband regarding the baby.

The abrupt termination of a pregnancy due to spontaneous abortion (miscarriage) or the sudden and unexpected death of the infant through stillbirth or neonatal problems brings a tragic halt to the months of happy anticipation. The dreams turn to harsh reality, the smiles to tears, and the wondrous movements of life to a painful void.

How do we as concerned professionals or friends help the mother of a lost child resolve her grief? How can we help her deal with the blow to her femininity and self-esteem? How do we help her reorganize her life? The ability to accomplish these complex, important tasks requires great empathy, understanding, sensitivity, and honest communication.

All too often the people the bereaved mother comes in contact with fail to provide her with the appropriate support following her loss. From the moment of her loss until many years later, numerous individuals will communicate their feelings and thoughts to her. These communications can range from a tear to a simple phrase, from the timeworn clichés of sympathy cards to long discussions. There will be moments of awkwardness and embarrassment, happiness and sadness, respect and contempt, anger and compassion. Regardless of the kind of communication exchanged, it is during these contacts with significant others that words and feelings are expressed that will have prolonged consequences for the emotional and mental health of the mother. It seems paradoxical that during these times when good communication is so essential, most people are ill-equipped to deal adequately with the situation.

Saying the right thing at the right time is a social skill few people possess. For many of us, saying the wrong thing at the wrong time is the norm. Such a blunder in communication, particularly in crucial, sensitive situations, leaves us questioning ourselves — Why did I say that? Why didn't I say this? Gosh, I hope I was understood! Likewise, due to the extreme emotional nature of the situation and the unexpectedness of infant death, we have to communicate with the mother in a most difficult time. Because we seldom practice such communication, our heartfelt feelings are often undermined by the words that we speak.

We find ourselves in many awkward circumstances where the proper words are difficult to find, yet the moment demands more than silence. For example, on meeting a friend who has been away for a year you ask, "How's your wife?" He responds, "Haven't you heard? We're divorced!" What do you say? "I'm sorry!" or "Congratulations!" or "What was the problem?" An awkward situation indeed, but some kind of response is necessary. So you struggle for the proper words, possibly committing an indiscretion, or you resign yourself to institutionalized responses such as "No, I didn't know," or "No, I haven't heard," and express little feeling, even though you may be deeply concerned. Regardless of the words spoken, the nonverbal cues may communicate shock, disbelief, or surprise, and leave the other person in the uncomfortable position of continuing the conversation.

Proper communication in such situations can be aided by understanding the situation and the feelings the other person is having. If you know, for example, that Joe is happy with his divorce, a response of "Gosh, I'm sorry to hear that," would be clearly inappropriate. On the other hand, the knowledge that Joe is upset about the demise of his marriage would hardly call for congratulations.

Fortunately, researchers during the past decade have provided information that makes it possible to gauge the feelings of persons experiencing grief. While feelings may vary from individual to individual, the information we have can serve as guidelines for communicating with the bereaved mother.

First of all, it is important to realize that the loss of her baby is a very real experience for the mother. It appears to matter very little whether the death is due to stillbirth, Sudden Infant Death Syn-

drome, neonatal death, or miscarriage. The mother of a five-month-old fetus experiences the same void as does the mother of a newborn child. The child has been part of her and she has grown to love it. In fact, the death of the baby can, in a sense, be viewed as the death of a part of the mother, a phenomenon called "maternal symbiosis." The death of an infant is a special kind of loss. It is easy to assume that since the child lives only a short time the loss can not be as traumatic as the death of an older child; however, this assumption is incorrect. If the loss is examined from a socio-psycho-biological viewpoint, death in infancy takes on a new dimension. From the moment of conception the infant draws its life from the body of the mother; it is dependent on her biological apparatus for its very existence. Likewise, the mother's biological system is altered and the child becomes an extension of her body from which she draws a certain degree of social and psychological nurture. As in other animal species, a relationship of symbiosis exists in which each organism thrives on the other. Because of this oneness, the death of an infant leaves the mother aching from a painful emptiness. Mothers describe this feeling as unlike any they have ever experienced; they may actually feel dead inside. The infant, as an extension of self, can no longer be seen or touched, nor can its movements be felt. Many times mothers will clutch their abdomens out of loss and their arms will ache to hold that part of themselves that died. Thus, the grief is often more intense and more lonely in this type of death than others, for the mother is the only person who has formed a relationship or bond with the dead child. Other people to whom the child has little identity — husband, physician, family, friends — may consider the death of the fetus or infant rather inconsequential compared to the death of an older person, but the mother cannot make this discrimination and consequently must suffer in a special way. The way she is treated, the understanding she receives, and the communications she encounters are all of utmost importance for her recovery.

With this introduction to the importance of proper communication and the nature of the mother-fetus-infant relationship, we now turn our attention to the grieving process and consider the kinds of communication that might be supportive or destructive to the mother during this critical emotional time. In the chapters that follow, we present a description of the mother's relationships with people who occupy significant positions during her time of grief: her husband, her physician, the hospital staff, friends, and relatives.

HUSBANDS AND WIVES

When unexpected fetal/infant death occurs, husbands and wives find themselves in a crisis situation unlike any they have had to face before. Because of a lack of institutionalized norms and social support systems, there are no externally prescribed patterns for their behavior. Because the loss of a baby is often their first encounter with the death of a family member, they have no previous experience from which to draw. Furthermore, the loss usually occurs in the early years of marriage before they, as a couple, have had to face many crises. Many times the fetal/infant death occurs during their first pregnancy. Thus, the stage is set for a real-life drama that has the potential for strengthening, but more often results in tearing apart, the affectional bonds between many husbands and wives.

The manner in which a couple deals with the myriad of problems they are sure to encounter can have a lasting effect on their marriage. Quite often, seemingly ideal relationships fall into disarray, resulting, at best, in feelings of bitterness and resentment — at worst, in separation or divorce. On the other hand, couples who outwardly appear on the brink of disaster, when faced with a crisis like fetal/infant death may actually draw closer together. It appears that regardless of the quality of the marriage before the loss, the aftermath of infant death brings either a positive or a negative change to the marriage.

While every couple has its own unique experiences, there are two major problem areas that most grieving husbands and wives have in common: communication and sexuality. Though it is true that these areas are common sources of difficulty for marriage in general, certain factors heighten their prevalence among couples who lose a baby.

Before specifically focusing on the problems of communication and sexuality, two factors that greatly contribute to these problem areas need to be understood: (1) the maternal and paternal bonding processes, and (2) the male and female sex roles.

MATERNAL BONDING

Perhaps no stronger affectional tie exists in the human species than that between mother and child. "Maternal love is a miraculous substance which God multiplies as he divides it," says Victor Hugo. "What are Raphael's Madonnas but the shadow of a mother's love, fixed in permanent outline forever?" asks Thomas Higgans. This special relationship has long been a favorite subject of artists, poets, philosophers, and historians.

Only in the past few decades, however, has the phenomenon of maternal love been brought under the searching eyes of science. What is the nature of the mother-infant bond? How does it develop? Answers to these questions have been sought through study of both human and other animal species. While the findings are voluminous, many of them have been integrated into a book entitled *Maternal-Infant Bonding*, by Marshall Klaus and John Kennell (Mosby, 1976). Not only have these authors presented us with a comprehensive review of previous research findings, they have also outlined a step-by-step process through which maternal-infant bonding occurs. This model can help us understand maternal grief.

Klaus and Kennell have outlined nine events that are importnat to the formation of a mother's attachment to her infant. They are (1) planning the pregnancy, (2) confirming the pregnancy, (3) accepting the pregnancy, (4) fetal movement, (5) accepting the fetus as an individual, (6) birth, (7) seeing the baby, (8) touching the baby, (9) giving care to the baby.

Planning the Pregnancy

The attachment of mother to infant often begins long before conception. Bonding, at least in fantasy, may begin as early as in childhood, when a young girl begins to fantasize about motherhood and to internalize the female sex role. Playing "house" and mothering dolls and younger siblings are activities that subconsciously begin to prepare her for motherhood.

As many women approach adulthood their thoughts often center on marriage and a family. For some, starting a family immediately after marriage is their goal. Others may begin a career and take time to adjust to marriage before planning children. Planning may simply involve abandonment of contraception, or it may include a scheduled sex life. In either case the woman makes a decision to get pregnant. Having a baby becomes a goal (for some, an obsession). The process of bonding has begun.

We do not mean to imply that planning is essential for bonding to occur, only that with planning it will most likely begin sooner. Many mothers who initially abhor the thought of pregnancy become fully bonded after the pregnancy is confirmed. As one mother of four told us, "None of our children was planned, but each was certainly welcomed."

Confirming the Pregnancy

Am I or am I not? Whether the baby is planned or unplanned,

this can be an anxiety-producing question. Some women fear an affirmative answer, others a negative one. In either case the confirmation of pregnancy is an important milestone. Those who have planned have accomplished their goal. Those to whom confirmation is a surprise experience a kaleidoscope of thoughts and emotions.

The initial realization of pregnancy under any circumstances can cause mixed feelings. The new mother-to-be reviews many facets of her life, ranging from her husband's projected reaction, to her own personal lifestyle. Economic considerations, marital situation, career, effect on other children, the reactions of her parents — each thought gradually leads to another crucial stage, acceptance of the pregnancy.

Acceptance of the Pregnancy

The new mother experiences two important developmental changes during pregnancy: (1) physical and emotional changes within herself, and (2) growth of the fetus. Feelings about these changes vary from woman to woman, depending on her desire to be pregnant and her present situation. During the early stages of pregnancy she must come to terms with the knowledge that she will soon be a mother. She must make sacrifices and must often drastically alter her lifestyle as she comes to accept the growing fetus as a real part of her self. For those who cannot accept their pregnancy, the bonding process ceases and abortion becomes an alternative. Notably, nearly one-third of all abortions performed in the United States involve married women.

Fetal Movement and Perception of the Fetus as a
Separate Individual

Fetal movement and perception of the fetus as a separate

individual often occur concurrently as "quickening," the sensa-
tion of fetal movement, making the mother-to-be aware that a baby
— another being — lives within her. The feeling of movement
requires the mother to change her concept of the fetus from a being
that is a part of herself to a living baby who will soon be a distinct
person. This realization prepares the woman for birth and physical
separation from her child. This preparedness, in turn, lays the
foundation for a permanent relationship with the child.

From quickening until birth the mother busies herself with
preparations for the new arrival — establishing a nursery, buying
clothes, attending baby showers. She also uses quiet moments of
reflection to fantasize about the baby, its sex, its appearance, its
personality. She begins to give the baby an identity and a name.
She may even talk to it or indirectly touch it by caressing her
abdomen. The baby becomes a third person "he" or "she" in
conversation. As the due-date approaches, the mother becomes
concerned about the infant's well-being, its normalcy, and the
ordeal of childbirth itself.

Birth, Seeing, and Touching the Baby

Seeing and touching the newly born baby completes the
bonding process and caretaking begins. Klaus and Kennell have
noted the importance of this period, what they refer to as the
"maternal-sensitive period," the first few minutes or hours after
birth. During this time the mother's attachment fully blossoms.
Events such as holding, touching, and just seeing the baby, will
have a lasting effect on the future development of the family.

This process of bonding has had a large impact on both
societal attitudes and childbirth practices in the United States.
"Natural" childbirth has become popular; "rooming in" hospital
arrangements are allowed; breast-feeding has again become fash-
ionable. Through all this, however, the bonding process between

the father and his infant has received little attention.

PATERNAL BONDING

According to Dr. Jim Menke, a Springfield, Illinois, neo-natologist, the father experiences essentially the same bonding process as does the mother, but it usually takes longer — sometimes becoming complete only when full caretaking begins. Much of the father's attachment, especially during the early stages of pregnancy, is intellectual. Frequently, however, the initial announcement of a positive pregnancy test elicits an emotional response from the father characterized sometimes by shock and disbelief, sometimes by fear and anxiety, and sometimes by surprise and happiness, and often by a combination of these feelings. Most frequently, the response also includes a great deal of pride. The specific emotional response usually depends on whether or not the pregnancy is a surprise or the result of planning. As his wife goes through the sometimes rather unpleasant physiological changes that accompany the early months of pregnancy, the husband becomes quite aware of an irritable, "crabby," impulsive companion, who is sometimes happy, sometimes moody, and often sick.

During this time a father may conduct a self-analysis, evaluating his life, reminiscing about the past, and projecting his future. This process, of which he may be unaware, may include a thorough review of his entire value structure. Where am I? Where have I been? Where am I going? What do I want from life? He considers his job and his professional aspirations, he assesses his relationship with friends, and he reflects on his marriage and family. Through this process he begins to realize that many adjustments will be necessary to accommodate and include the expected new arrival. He begins to anticipate feeding and clothing the baby, paying medical bills for the child, educating the child, supporting the child, altering his routine, and adjusting to his new role of father. His first realization of these new responsibilities may prove to be overwhelming.

Perhaps the first sign of emotional bonding in the father begins with fetal movement. Being able to feel the kicking in his wife's stomach adds a sudden reality to the father's thoughts. Because the process of bonding for the father usually doesn't begin until this time, he has a great deal of "catching up" to do with his wife, who has already developed a deep emotional attachment to the growing infant within her.

Through the remaining months of pregnancy the feelings of attachment may grow, but they seldom reach the intense level of bonding that his wife has developed with the child. He becomes an onlooker as she prepares for the coming birth, and sometimes he becomes lost in the shuffle as she becomes the center of attention of family and friends. He may anticipate the birth with anxiety or fear for his wife's well-being. The mother-to-be focuses all her emotional energies on the coming delivery and her baby; the father's emotions are split between anticipation of a healthy infant and concern for his wife.

Full bonding of father and child may in fact not occur until birth is complete. When the child is born and his wife is safe, caretaking begins. As one father put it:

I really had very little in the way of feelings about the baby. I mean I felt him kicking in Jane's stomach, but it really wasn't "real" to me. I had no conception of its sex or anything like that. But when the nurse brought this little bundle into the waiting room and said, "Mr. Stevens, would you like to see your son?" he became a reality. When I saw this little guy, the feelings of attachment were overpowering!

Male and Female Sex Roles

One additional variable, reinforcing the different reactions to a loss, which deserves mentioning at this point, is the social expectations attached to the roles of men and women in our society. One man, whose wife delivered a stillborn girl, expressed it this way:

> I had to be strong. Right away they were bombarding me with questions about this and that. Everyone was encouraging me to be composed when I talked with Nancy. I was told not to show any emotion because it would upset her. It's funny: I was hurting too, but I was not expected to show it.

While there are many obvious changes occurring in sex roles in today's society, the social roles of father and mother, of man and woman, have by tradition been sharply defined. Socially pre-scribed behaviors, usually learned early in life, often manifest themselves in response to infant death. A woman is expected to provide emotional support and comfort through learned female traits. By contrast, a male has been assigned traits that are designed to give him a mental and emotional edge in a highly competitive society. Thus, women are viewed as nurturing, affectionate, dependent, passive, expressive, and so forth. Men, on the other hand, are expected to be achievement oriented, reserved, aggressive, strong, independent, and nonexpressive.

These roles can influence greatly the overt reactions of both husbands and wives in stressful situations. Wives are not only allowed to show, but are expected to show, a great outpouring of emotion. The husband, on the other hand, must remain "strong" and protective of his wife, an unfortunate cultural dictate that often leads to suppression of his own grief. Just as bonding is accom-plished at different rates, the grief process is in many instances incongruous also. The husband and wife may find themselves operating in different stages of the grief process. Again, this incongruence may foster problems.

MARITAL CONFLICTS

While every case has its unique characteristics, it appears that incongruent bonding and incongruent grieving, in combination with each other, underlie most marital conflicts following infant death. Although tensions abound and conflicts erupt, many couples are either unaware of the sources of their disagreements or, when they are aware, they do not fully understand them.

While the mother has become very involved with the baby, the father has yet to develop an emotional attachment. If early miscarriage occurs, the mother feels a sense of loss; the father only disappointment. She, on the one hand, cannot understand why he isn't upset; he, on the other hand, cannot understand why she is. Often the husband will take a position of "That's tough, we can try again," not fully appreciating the significance of the loss to the mother. This uninformed and unintentional mistake can lead to great feelings of bitterness and resentment in his wife. Later, as grief begins to subside, they reflect upon the previous tumultuous times and realize that they were victims of a common process over which they had little control — a process that can lead to a complete breakdown in communication.

Based upon our interviews, we have developed an explanation of husband-wife conflict that can be used to grasp a basic understanding of what frequently occurs following fetal/infant death. We should state at this point that many couples do not experience discord; in fact, many couples find their relationships strengthened by this unfortunate event. Examples of such positive outcomes will be discussed toward the end of this chapter.

Basically, the process proceeds as follows: conception takes place and the pregnancy is confirmed. Unknowingly, the couple's bonding process occurs at a different rate, causing a difference in the emotional attachment of the mother and father to the infant. Depending upon when death occurs, the parents will experience the loss in different ways. Each spouse reacts as society prescribes — the mother expresses her emotions, the father remains composed. The father's unemotional reaction to an early miscarriage may reflect his true feelings; he has yet to develop an attachment to the child. In cases of stillbirth, he may experience a sense of loss, but not to the extent that his wife does. With neonatal loss, the father will grieve, but in fulfillment of his social role, his emotions remain hidden. In either type of loss he becomes his wife's protector. Seeing only his rational side, his wife may develop feelings of bitterness and resentment. She interprets his lack of an emotional display as a lack of concern for their loss.

When the father finally does acknowledge his feelings of loss, he finds few outlets for expression and little social support. The attentions of friends and family are focused on his wife. Thus, the husband finds himself isolated; he can't express his feelings to his wife because of the protector role he is forced into, and he can't express them to family and friends because their attentions are focused on the mother. Isolated and alone, he, too, may develop feelings of bitterness. Communication channels between him and his wife close; other problems are then perpetuated.

This process seems to recur in case after case. The following sections describe how it begins and operates with each type of loss.

Miscarriage

Problems between husbands and wives in case of early miscarriage most often result directly from the incongruent bonding process. The mother, having begun the attachment process, feels the significance of her loss. The father, not yet having begun the bonding process, may view it as little more than a disappointment. As one young father related to us:

My wife miscarried at three months when I was in my second year of

---
77

medical school. Due to the irregularity of her periods, she hadn't even confirmed the pregnancy yet. She suspected from the symptoms, but she had not told me. Therefore, I had no knowledge of it. She was very upset about the miscarriage, but I had no feeling of loss. I couldn't understand why she was so upset, and she couldn't understand why I wasn't. I just wanted to forget about it, but she wouldn't.

And from his wife:

He treated this like nothing had happened. I wanted this pregnancy so bad. We had been trying for a long time, and I knew we had finally succeeded. It seemed as if he just didn't care. I think I really resented that. He simply didn't understand.

For this couple incongruent bonding resulted in communication problems. Fortunately, within a year they became parents of a healthy young son. Other couples, however, are not as fortunate; they experience one failure after another. They may experience two, three, or four conceptions — but no baby. Their losses lead to frustration and feelings of inadequacy as men and women. Tensions rise; communication ceases; marital problems often ensue. Left unexpressed, their feelings are manifested in many ways — from a decrease in social activity to problems in sexuality. After three unsuccessful pregnancies Jeanne expressed her feelings this way:

After the third loss I began to have doubts about myself. I began to wonder if I had the ability to produce a healthy baby. When the same complications arose in the fourth pregnancy, I just about fell apart. I felt like the world's biggest failure. I became a social recluse; paranoid in fact! I thought everyone looked at me as a failure. It affected my relationship with my in-laws and it hurt my marriage. I let myself go and took no pride in my appearance. I think it was a subconscious attempt to sabotage our sex life. You see, I connected sex with pregnancy and I couldn't risk another failure.

Spontaneous abortions in the later stages of pregnancy may

heighten many feelings and emotions. The following comments come from interviews with a young California couple whose twins aborted in the fifth month of pregnancy. Lisa said:

> Our problems really stemmed from three sources. First of all, we didn't plan the pregnancy. David was a bit upset that I was pregnant and we hadn't been able to plan it. I guess I felt like I had let him down. We hadn't violated any of our birth control methods. It was just a disappointment in not being able to plan it. I think that I started to get irritated at his reaction to the news of the pregnancy. I became very attached to them [the twins]. When I lost them, two things happened that were, and still are, hard to take. The first was while I was in the hospital. I wasn't really aware of what was going on around me. Mostly I thought it was a nightmare and that I would wake up. But then I felt my stomach and it was flat. When I asked to see the twins both my husband and the nurse said no! I finally got to see them but not to touch them. I never got to say goodbye. Later on I knew I had made a mistake. But David . . . David didn't even look at them. It was like he denied they existed. After we got home, and to this day, he refers to it as a miscarriage! I know the medical community didn't consider them to be human beings yet . . . and neither did David. But they were people to me, they were part of me. I felt them moving. It was more than a miscarriage; I lost babies and that is very different. He just wouldn't talk about them. I felt as though they were his babies too. I think that maybe he wanted to maintain a detachment so he could be a Rock of Gibraltar for me to fall apart on. He was afraid to talk because it would upset me. He didn't know he was upsetting me more by not talking about them.

David, Lisa's husband said:

> It has put a real strain on our relationship. Ever since we were married we had shared experiences and had done things together. At that time I was very involved in work. My career was just beginning to bloom and I wasn't ready for the news of the pregnancy. After Lisa told me she was pregnant I guess I felt like I just wasn't ready. At any rate I wasn't enthusiastic about it. I had wanted to wait another year or so. After they died I saw that Lisa was greatly affected. I have to admit that I was becoming more excited about fatherhood, but it didn't affect me as much as it did her. Anyway, the next few weeks were difficult. I could dive into my work and my new activities. I had distractions but Lisa had none. She

was really pulled down. To help her I didn't mention the twins or, when forced to, I would try to minimize the loss. I know now that that was a mistake.

With this young couple, incongruent bonding, incongruent grieving, the protective role of the husband, and the lack of communication had a great impact on their marriage. David's refusal to see the twins and involvement in his career enabled him to deny and suppress his feelings. As protector, he minimized the loss by acknowledging only a "miscarriage." Lisa not only grieved alone but also began to feel hostile and resentful that no one would recognize the significance of her loss. As she so aptly put it, "It was more than a miscarriage; I lost babies, and that is very different."

Stillbirth

Although incongruent bonding is still the basic source of husband-wife conflicts, stillbirths create special problems. As the birth date approaches, the baby quits moving and no fetal heartbeat can be heard. The couple then faces hours or days anticipating the birth of a dead infant and their problems often begin.

The mother, being almost fully bonded with her baby, may begin the grief process even before delivery. The father, anxiously awaiting a new family member, will also experience a great feeling of loss. Rather than grieve, however, he submits to societal dictates; he becomes the protector. He shields his wife from the harsh reality of stillbirth by offering comments designed to ease her feelings, but often they only serve to further the process of denial: "Maybe he's just sleeping"; "Maybe they've made a mistake." This well-intentioned encouragement may only postpone the inevitable encounter with reality.

Even before delivery, particularly in cases of natural childbirth, the husband sometimes faces a major decision — a decision that most appropriately should be his wife's to make. Should she be sedated or not? The obstetrician seeks his advice, or sometimes he might give an unsolicited opinion. Often the decision is made with no consultation with the mother. The result may be contrary to her wishes, and the seed of future problems is sown. The wife, wanting to experience childbirth, wants to be alert; the husband, wanting to protect her from agony, requests sedation; the results are sometimes disastrous. Such was the case with Linda and Tom. From Tom's perspective:

> I really thought it was the best thing for her. The O.B. couldn't be certain about what the baby might look like. Given Linda's emotional state at the time, I didn't think she could handle the shock of any gross abnormalities. My concern at that moment was totally for my wife.

Despite the fact that Linda knew why the decision was made, she neither accepted nor appreciated it. As she related to us:

> I didn't care what they thought. It was my body and my baby. I fought it as long as I could but when labor got hard I guess I just gave in. When I woke up in my room I felt a tremendous emptiness and a great deal of anger. I still haven't completely forgiven Tom for that.

In other cases, labor commences, birth occurs, and the quiet reality of stillbirth can no longer be avoided. Through all of this the husband, the protector and rational decision maker, finds that he must suppress his own grief, at least temporarily. He becomes his wife's link to the outside world. Controlling visitors and news about the loss, he allows no one to get to her except through him. By assuming this position, he continues to suppress his own feelings of grief. Others perceive him as strong; they feel that "he must be doing O.K."

During this same period of time, he may, in a sincere effort to make it as easy on his wife as possible, assume the responsibility of making many difficult, but necessary, decisions. Naming the baby? Autopsy or not? Funeral arrangements? Dismantling the nursery? Each of these is an important consideration. As a general rule, the father seldom makes the right decision unless he has first consulted his wife.

While every decision during this critical period is an important one, perhaps none is more important for the stability of the husband-wife relationship than the question of whether or not to see the stillborn baby. A mother who is not allowed to see her baby often develops feelings of anger and resentment toward those who have denied her that privilege. Just as important for their relationship, however, is the husband's attitude and willingness to share this experience. Quite often he refuses. This sometimes evokes an unanticipated reaction from his wife, as this young woman's comments illustrate:

> I asked him to see the baby but he just wouldn't do it. I remember I felt so angry. It was a denial of our son — a denial of his love for both the baby and me.

The importance of sharing this experience goes beyond simple recognition of the loss. Momentarily, at least, it gives the couple a chance to grieve together. Without this mutual experience, the grief process will remain disjointed and communication will remain strained. Although the husband essentially remains the pillar of strength, his patience and strength eventually reach their limits. Although he sometimes can find emotional outlets with others, anger frequently erupts, anger vented toward his wife. Michael was described by his wife as being extremely supportive for the first few months after she delivered a stillborn girl. But as he told us:

> After we came home we really didn't want people around us. I guess we just wanted to crawl up in our own little world and pull the blankets over

us. I would say this had a big impact on us. We talked about it. I listened to Rita day after day. She really wanted an answer to why she had lost our daughter. She kept on and on. After three months I decided I had had enough. Our lives had to change. One night I told her that I simply didn't want to talk about it any more. She became very hostile because I was the only one who could understand. I just plain cut her off from any more talk about it. As brutal as it may seem, I had had enough. We had to get on with living.

Neonatal Death

In cases of a live birth the husband very quickly reaches the same level of attachment as his wife. They have shared the birth and, many times, the death. They should be able to begin the process of grieving together. Ironically, however, neonatal loss brings about a type of role reversal of mother and father, creating some rather unique circumstances. Newborn babies who are "in trouble" are often separated from their mother shortly after birth. They are transferred to high risk or special care nurseries, sometimes many miles from the hospital in which the birth occurred. While the mother recuperates, the father follows the baby to the new location. His caretaking begins; he becomes fully bonded to the child, and he establishes a relationship with a live baby — his baby!

During this time, pressures on the father are tremendous. He anxiously awaits the hour by hour reports and watches the progress or decline in his child's condition. Usually he is alone. If the infant survives for several days, the stress becomes greater. Job responsibilities must be met. If he has other children he assumes household and childcare duties. He is also the constant liaison with his wife. Back and forth he goes, constantly shuttling from home to work to wife to baby and back home again. As one husband said, "I never felt so torn in so many directions as I felt during those eight days."

And when the baby dies, what does he feel? How does he react? Quite obviously, he grieves. He is torn with emotion: anger, resentment, and even guilt. How does he react? The way he is expected to, of course.

Often, his grief cannot be expressed openly. He may find a quiet place to be alone and cry for his lost child. But he soon gains composure and faces the tasks of telling his wife — of assuming the protector role — and of making the necessary decisions. Through all this, he, too, is deeply hurt. He, too, needs support and comfort. Frequently, however, support for the father is not to be found. He plays his role well, he is perceived as strong, and he is essentially forgotten. Attention and concern are focused on his wife. The case of Alex is typical:

I really wanted a boy. He was prematurely born and weighed only two pounds. They transferred him to Stanford and a Special Care Nursery where he was put on a respirator. He died six days later from a collapsed lung. During that time I had minute by minute progress reports and had decided the chances were slim. There were a lot of sad feelings, some anger, pain, and regret. I wanted a boy! The birth had been by Caesarean and Judy had stayed in Memorial Hospital. You can't imagine how lonely I felt. I was bitter at our parents for not coming to see my son. I desperately wished that someone had been there with me. For about an hour after they told me I tried to gain some composure, then I went to tell Judy. That was really hard, very tough. She had not been allowed to see the baby.

I was cast into the typical male role. The feelings I had were primarily loneliness and anger because I had to bear this thing by myself. That really came to surface later when Judy came home from the hospital. I was cast into the male role of having to be this pillar of strength and supply all the necessary support for Judy. Not once was I ever patted on the back or talked to. No one said we understand that you are having the same kind of hurts or how are you doing? I developed tremendous feelings of anger at everybody, including Judy. Our relationship suffered greatly and eventually led to a separation.

We heard essentially the same thing from a father in Texas:

After the baby died there was a steady stream of friends and relatives through the house. I couldn't tell them to get the hell out, that we wanted to be alone. I kept hearing how I had to give Phyllis all the necessary support, keep a macho image! I finally heard that I shouldn't feel bad about losing the baby, that Phyllis was more important now! That really hit hard. At no time did anyone show any concern about how I was doing. I've learned since then that Phyllis tried, but at the time she was lost in the physical pain of surgery [Caesarian] and the mental anguish of having lost the baby. She also had to put up a front for the relatives. It all tore us apart at that time when we needed to be the closest. We needed to be able to express our feelings to each other, but everyone was in the way.

This break in communication had the following results:

I wasn't able to handle it at the time. The only thing I thought about was how badly I hurt. It was my baby, too! I became more and more angry. Eventually I vented my anger at Phyllis. Instead of wanting to comfort her . . . I wanted to hurt her. It all culminated in my involvement with a girl at work who would listen to my feelings. It was a combination of my angry feelings and the desire to be with someone who would let me express how I felt. When I would go home I would remember how I had to be "strong." With her I found comfort.

These cases are not the norm. But they do illustrate the sometimes disastrous effects that infant death can have on a marriage. It's unfortunate that society denies the father his right to express pain by isolating him and forgetting that it was his loss, too.

More often than not, the mother recognizes what is happening but feels helpless to do anything about it. One young mother did the only thing she could think of, given her condition.

I saw what was happening to Ken and I felt for him. One morning I sneaked down to the gift shop, bought a small box of candy, and put it under my pillow. When visiting hours came I gave it to him and simply said "I love you . . . I know what you're going through." With that we cried together for the first time.

The benefits of this simple expression of understanding, when contrasted with the enormous problems it may have prevented, are inestimable.

PREVENTING MARITAL CONFLICT

Thus far, we have examined several sources of husband-wife conflict and looked at a number of cases in which problems developed. How can such unfortunate outcomes be prevented? How can couples presently involved in situations such as these successfully work through their problems? At the beginning of this chapter we stated that many marriages are strengthened as the spouses work through their period of mourning. We believe that through an analysis of such positive outcomes, answers to these questions can be found.

In one case that was very similar to that of the young Texas couple discussed in the previous section, marital separation actually occurred. As the husband told us:

> I left for three months. During this time I only saw her on a couple of occasions. She recognized the communication problems at the time, but I couldn't see them. We decided to see a counselor. When I came back it was like walking on eggshells for awhile, but finally we realized we had to open the communication channels. Once we tried, it seemed like a lot of doors opened up so easily. We became husband and wife again.

During the course of our research, we heard many couples allude to the "strengthening" of their relationship after the loss of their baby. Some of these couples allowed their loss to become a positive force in their lives, as the following two cases illustrate.

> We quickly realized that no one else could really understand the pain that the two of us felt. We decided that despite the rough spots we would face this thing together . . . in the same way we did the pregnancy. I think the prenatal classes helped us a lot. Together we learned what to expect as far

as the birth was concerned, but we also got to know each other better. He understood my moods and, I guess you would say, we learned how to talk. After we lost the baby [stillbirth] the experience in communication that we had gotten from the classes was so important. We could sit and talk about our feelings and cry together if we wanted to. But we could also talk about the positive aspects of the situation . . . the good things we had.

Another couple whose son lived for eleven days took a similar approach:

Todd's death brought us closer together. We conceived him together, shared in his birth, enjoyed our eleven days with him together, and then grieved together. We talked about it a lot and we cried a lot. But we also realized that in his short life he had given us so much happiness despite his condition. After we buried him we left town for a week and splurged. We did things that we had always wanted to do but kept putting off. I guess it was a catharsis but it was beneficial to us. Even though it may sound as if we were running, that wasn't the case at all. Todd was very much with us. I might add, too, that during those eleven days we gathered as much information as possible. Being informed helped us to understand and deal with the crisis and the result that we knew was coming. We shared in every way possible the entire experience.

A comparison of these cases with those with negative consequences points to several areas of importance: (1) "sharing" the pregnancy, (2) "sharing" the loss, (3) being informed, and (4) communicating. Positive outcomes are probable among those couples who can avoid the pitfalls they encounter from the time of conception through grief resolution. As we study the effects on husbands and wives we can see several obvious contrasts:

Positive Outcomes	*Negative Outcomes*
Pregnancy planned	Pregnancy unplanned
Both spouses involved in all aspects of pregnancy	Father detached from pregnancy

Both spouses informed about childbirth	One or both spouses uninformed about childbirth
Both spouses feel free to express emotion	One or both spouses reluctant to express emotion
Grieve together	Grieve separately
Find time to be alone	Find little time to be alone
Overcome societal dictates	Submit to societal dictates
Look for positives	Dwell on negatives
Communicate	Do not communicate
Empathetic with each other's feelings	Self-centered

Many couples who have lost a baby may be presently faced with a breakdown in communication and one or more of its attendant problems. For these couples we offer the following suggestions from our sources as well as others:

1. Try to open the channels by yourselves. Remember that you have dealt with other crises together. Why not this one? As you both disclose your feelings, the burden you carry alone will gradually diminish. She is your wife. He is your husband. Trust that she/he will try to understand. Although others can help you, ultimately you must help yourselves.

2. In addition, it is vital that ground rules for grieving be developed. This should be done together and individually. Each spouse should feel secure that what they do together as a couple and individually is right and normal for them.

3. Rejoice in the days when your marriage feels safe and secure. As you regain some of your old patterns, some may remain disrupted and awkward. Have patience as you learn to take risks with loving deeply again.

4. See a trained professional. Many physicians, counselors, social workers, and psychologists are trained in third-party listen-

ing. They can help you understand and clarify your jumbled thoughts and feelings. Once clarified they become easier to express. Objective listeners can also point out things that you find difficult to see in your present emotional and/or mental state.

5. Find other parents who have lost a baby. In many ways, others who have experienced a loss can help you. Believe it or not, you might help them, too! Unlike others, they can understand your feelings. They have been there! You'll often find that many of those "abnormal" thoughts or feelings you have are really quite normal. In many communities there are organized parent support groups. You'll find a list of some of them in this book. If no group exists in your community, you may want to start one (see a later chapter for some tips). If you are less ambitious we can promise you that another couple will not be hard to find. You probaby won't have to look further than your own block.

Many of our readers may have recently lost an infant and now find themselves in a stage of crisis. In this critical period when emotions and confusions abound, there are numerous things you can do and others you can avoid doing that can help now and/or prevent future problems. To husbands we offer the following suggestions:

1. Say, to hell with what they say. The unexpressive male is a product of a legal-rational world. This is a time for emotion. Let your feelings out! Whatever they might be, they are your feelings, they are valid, and they need to be expressed.

2. Crying does not invalidate manliness. It's much easier to play the expected role than it is to deviate. You might say that it takes a man to let others see you cry.

3. Let your wife know you care. Let her know that you care not only about her — but also about the baby. It is significant for her. She wants to know that it is also important to you.

4. Take or make time to be alone with her. Both of you need

some time to steady yourselves before you have to cope with outside pressures and demands. This time can also get your grieving processes "in tune" with each other.

5. Include your wife in decision making. Not only will it lessen your responsibilities, but it may also prevent future problems. Most often she wants to be included; exclusion may facilitate bitterness and resentment.

6. Realize that other people simply do not understand you. Others are caught in the same cultural orientation that you are. Their comments to you have no malicious intent. Either let them know that you hurt, too, or ignore them.

7. Remember that you have rights. You may be led to believe that options are unavailable to you. Assert yourself! You have many choices: names, photos, seeing and holding, autopsies, funeral arrangements, and many more. Find out what they are.

8. Establish good communications with your wife. Nothing you can do is more important.

Mothers may find these suggestions helpful:

1. Grieve in your own way. Grieve whenever and however you want; your reactions are normal and necessary. Allow yourself this privilege.

2. Exercise your rights as a patient. You have many of them. There are very few inflexible hospital "policies." Make your desires known and stand your ground.

3. Carefully consider all decisions regarding the baby. Though many decisions may seem inconsequential at the time, you may later have second thoughts and regret snap decisions.

4. Try to look behind your husband's facade. Remember that he is expected to play a protective role, but he may be hurting, too. Acknowledge his sometimes forgotten feelings.

5. Do not feel socially obligated to anyone. This is your loss.

You need not play hostess to relatives and friends, particularly at the expense of time with your husband.

Perhaps you are now pregnant or are planning to become pregnant. If so, there are several preventive measures you can take now to avoid the trouble should problems occur. As we have seen, the problems of husbands and wives often begin early in the pregnancy. Though few in number, these "tips" may prove to be helpful.

1. Try to plan the pregnancy. Though surprises can be pleasant, actively planning a pregnancy facilitates communication and fosters a "team" spirit.

2. Share the pregnancy. Too often pregnancy is viewed as strictly a woman's concern. Nothing could be further from the truth; both of you should be involved from conception through delivery. You can find classes in prepared childbirth in most communities.

One final suggestion: regardless of the stage of pregnancy or grief — keep informed! Knowledge about pregnancy, fetal development, abnormal conditions, available options — everything — can help to overcome many doubts, fears, and anxieties.

Pregnancy can be a positive, sharing, binding force in the lives of young couples, or it can be disruptive. The same is true with infant death. It can be either strengthening or separating. Through open communication and sharing, you can make the best of it.

EFFECTS ON SEXUALITY

Sex was much more intense during the whole ordeal. It was like we were trying to compensate. You put much more of yourself into giving to the other person. Lovemaking became much more intense . . . more tender . . . in both frequency and feeling.

He wouldn't touch me, not even kiss me, let alone have intercourse. It was repulsive for him to hold me. It became a "you stay on your side, I'll stay on mine," understanding. I think that maybe I started to test him. The more he resisted, the more I wanted him. Finally I quit trying and the resentment set in.

From the experiences of these two women, the wide variation in the effects of fetal/infant death on sexuality becomes apparent. In the first case (a neonatal loss) the sexual relationship was strengthened, in the second (a stillbirth) it deteriorated. Though these may be extreme examples, it is obvious that the tragedy of fetal/infant death alters this most intimate dimension of the husband-wife relationship.

For some couples the sexual relationship is enriched. A positive effect results when sex becomes an extension of the communication and mutual support that the couple establishes during the days and weeks following their loss. For these couples, sexuality becomes an expression of their love, affection, and support for each other.

For other couples, the sexual relationship suffers. Both men and women can experience a diminished sex drive due primarily to symptoms of grief. Often the loss of self-esteem that accompanies maternal grief leads to a decrease in sexual attractiveness. Guilt may cause either partner (or both) to disallow pleasure for themselves. Still other couples may call a halt to sexual activity due to their fear of another pregnancy. Finally, whereas some couples fear pregnancy, others become obsessed with it. Their sex life becomes scheduled and mechanical. While increasing in frequency, it lacks intimacy and quality.

Often these effects on sexuality appear soon after the loss and are relatively short-lived; but frequently, they arise months later, often with disastrous effects on the marital relationship.

This chapter examines the most common alterations to the sexual activity of grieving parents. They can be summarized as follows:

Type of Change	*Reasons for Change*
Positive (Increase in sexual response and activity)	Expression of affection and intimacy Compensation for the loss Desire to conceive another child
Negative (Decrease in sexual response and activity)	Fear of pregnancy Obsession with getting pregnant Loss of self-confidence Disallowance of personal pleasure Loss of sex drive

Affection and Intimacy

Perhaps one positive outcome of the social isolation imposed on grieving parents is the strengthened affectional ties that develop between some husbands and wives. As the community withdraws from them, these couples find comfort in each other. Intimacy, expression of feeling, and affection increase, and their sexual relationship is enriched. In effect they are, by circumstances, driven into each other's arms. Lovemaking takes on a new dimension. Each spouse is drawn to the other in a more intimate and passionate way than ever before.

The comment at the beginning of this chapter, "Lovemaking became much more intense, more tender, in both frequency and feeling," is very representative of this positive effect. However, as with any compensatory coping mechanism, a word of caution is in order. It is important for couples to recognize that expression of grief, following their loss, is essential. Couples that can grieve together and find comfort in each other's arms may reach the resolution of their grief more quickly than couples that grow apart. However, if sexual activity becomes a substitute for, or an escape from, other normal adjustment patterns, it may serve only to repress or delay the more negative manifestations of the grieving process.

Compensation for Loss

Another positive change affecting sexuality following the death of an infant is found in the use of sex as a compensation for the loss. This is defined as a positive change because it involves the "giving" of oneself to the other person. For a period of time following the loss, sexual expression may become particularly intense as both husband and wife try to make up for their loss. The giving of one another in the sexual encounter has several positive benefits: it creates an atmosphere in which intensive communication can take place; it reduces the feelings of isolation experienced by the sometimes negative or neutral responses of friends and relatives; and it releases the tension created by the hectic circumstances of the loss itself.

Compensation for the loss through increased sexual response and activity carries a positive effect only so long as the activity is accompanied by genuine feelings of affection and intimacy. It should not be used as a psychological form of punishment, i.e., "I will surrender myself; I will give of myself because I cannot give anything else!" Under these conditions, compensation takes the form of a negative activity that is sure to have unanticipated results. Particularly for the wife, such a reaction can eventually result in an intensification of feelings of failure, guilt, and inadequacy.

Where there is a genuine feeling of affection and the need to share an intimate experience with a loved and respected spouse, increased sexuality can have a very positive effect as a way of softening the impact of fetal/infant death and of compensating, in part, for the loss of the parental role.

Desire to Conceive

The desire to conceive, as a positive change, must be placed in opposition to the "obsession to become pregnant again" that will be discussed in the following section. For a couple involved in family planning, the desire to conceive again, following a loss, can be a positive attitude if their desire is tempered with rationality and forethought. Admonishments from friends and relatives, such as "You're crazy if you try again," or "Forget it; if you want children, adopt them," should be ignored. If the couple genuinely wants a baby, the desire to conceive can have a positive influence on their sexual relationship. It can also contribute greatly to the resolution of grief.

Taking steps to become pregnant is a positive goal for the couple; it increases their sexual activity and creates many psychological benefits. For example, it may reduce the element of uncertainty when the ability to create a healthy baby is questioned; it may bring out into the open deep-seated feelings of fear and anxiety where they can be dealt with on a rational basis; or it may give the couple a positive goal for which to strive, reducing the feeling of "drifting" about with little sense of direction.

Fear of Pregnancy

One of the most fascinating aspects of the changing sexual relationship after fetal/infant loss is the psychological connection that many couples make between sex and pregnancy. In simple terms, to many couples sex means baby. They view pregnancy as an inevitable outcome of sexual activity; therefore, they say, "let's not indulge!"

The fear of pregnancy, with its subsequent decrease in sexual activity, usually stems from one of two sources. The most common is simply the fear of experiencing another loss. A second concern relates to feelings of inadequacy on the part of one or both spouses. This latter source of stress is quite common among couples in their second marriage. This situation will be discussed shortly.

The fear of another pregnancy leading to another loss was a "reason" for a decrease in sexual activity for Jeff and Gwynn, a young Florida couple who lost a prematurely born daughter. From Jeff's perspective:

> Gwynn was greatly affected by the loss of our daughter. We went through several weeks of pure hell. She spent many hours just sitting and crying. No one was able to give us a satisfactory answer about why Jennifer [their daughter] had the difficulties that she had. Given the severe reaction that Gwynn had, I really felt hesitant to try again until I could be assured that this wouldn't happen again.

Gwynn expressed a similar attitude:

> At first, after the usual six weeks waiting, I really felt like resuming our sex life. However, as we sought an answer as to why Jennifer had died, I began to question my ability to produce a healthy baby. I really became afraid of sex. I didn't want to go through that again.

Despite their weakened sexual relationship, Jeff and Gwynn were able to share their feelings. Such is not always the case. Often one partner will make the "silent" decision to avoid pregnancy and, at the same time, attribute the opposite motive to the spouse. Most often this is the strategy of the husband. These comments from Steve illustrate a common response from men:

> I felt like Jan wanted another baby, but I didn't see how she could handle another loss. I wanted to wait until she adjusted to this one, so I thought it best to limit our sexual activity.

The psychological connection these couples attach to sex and pregnancy is fascinating indeed. Obviously, proper use of contraceptive techniques would minimize the chances of conception, yet many husbands and wives forego contraception even when their religious beliefs permit it. Others who do practice contraceptive methods still harbor a tremendous fear of pregnancy.

This may be an especially stressful situation for husbands and wives in second marriages, particularly if their present spouse had healthy children in a previous marriage. They rationalize that because their spouse previously had a healthy baby, then they must be the inadequate partner. Consequently, they fear another pregnancy, and they avoid sexual activity.

Obsession with Getting Pregnant

While many couples diminish their sexual activity following a loss, others become obsessed with conceiving another child. The following comments are illustrative of the nature of this activity:

> We literally turned sex off and on per schedule. I really didn't like it much at all. Sex lost all spontaneity. With the infertility problems that we had, we were put on schedules. It was so difficult to have a "feeling" kind of relationship when you had to look at a calendar and say, "Well — today or not?" That was a real problem.

Some even became obsessed with replacing their lost son or daughter with a baby of the same sex:

> Sex? I read this thing about choosing the sex of your child. I couldn't understand why he wanted to wait, when I wanted so desperately to replace the baby I had lost. Until I conceived it was pretty much just being a baby machine. You see, I wanted a daughter and this article said that in order to get a girl a woman should not have an orgasm. So, I simply lay there like a machine.

As a final example of this obsession, Christy told us, "Sex became so mechanical — just to have a baby. There wasn't much feeling, even about who the father was."

While conception and delivery of a new, healthy baby is probably the greatest healer of maternal grief, medical opinion is divided regarding how soon after the loss conception should be attempted. Some professionals suggest that couples should try as soon as they feel like it. Others recommend waiting for an extended period to allow for grief resolution. Regardless of which direction the couple takes, the important consideration is that the mother realizes that the new baby is indeed a different baby.

Many mothers take too little time before they attempt another pregnancy. They do not consider their psychological or emotional readiness, nor do they think about whether a new baby is a different baby or a replacement for the one they lost. They become obsessed with the idea of pregnancy, desperately trying to fill the emptiness caused by their loss. The effect this behavior has on the sexual relationship can be very detrimental. The intensity of sex increases greatly, yet intimacy, affection, and spontaneity decrease. This problem appears to be most prevalent among those couples who have experienced previous fertility problems. As both John and Renée stated, "Sex became very scheduled." Sex loses it intimacy and becomes purely a vehicle for pregnancy.

Loss of Self-Confidence

The loss of a baby can be devastating to self-confidence and self-esteem, particularly in cases of multiple losses. This lack of confidence and esteem often manifests itself in sexual matters. Sometimes women, to avoid another pregnancy, will deliberately sabotage the sexual relationship. In other cases, decreased ego leads to a lack of desire to be sexually attractive. In either case, the result is the same — the sexual relationship suffers. Rather than try to make themselves attractive, "anti-sex" partners may unconsciously make themselves unappealing. Weight gain, unkempt appearance, crude speech, and other detracting characteristics are often adopted, without the recognition that such behavior may be defenses against sexual involvement.

After two miscarriages, Kay related the following:

I felt like the world's biggest failure. In social gatherings, I felt like everyone knew what had happened and looked at me as someone who could not produce a healthy baby. Eventually, I quit going out. I would stay home all day, I began overeating, and I generally took little pride in my appearance. After a period of time, my relationship with Mike began to suffer, but it didn't bother me. I was so afraid of getting pregnant and going through the whole ordeal again.

From Kay's husband:

Effect on sex? Definitely! This had a tremendous effect on Kay's self concept. She really went downhill. She just didn't take care of herself. Though it's tough to say, she became less appealing to me because she had no confidence in herself. To her, having sex meant having another child.

Disallowing Personal Pleasure

Perhaps, as a means of compensation for their loss, or maybe out of feelings of guilt, couples will often diminish their sexual activities as a form of self-punishment, to disallow themselves any personal pleasures. As Laura explained:

After Joey died, I felt it was bad to feel good. That may sound rather funny, but I simply would not allow myself any self-indulgences, fun, or pleasure. My interest in sex especially decreased. I became very unresponsive for a period of several months. It wasn't until we decided to try to have another child that I regained any interest in sex.

Laura's orientation toward sexuality is a rather common form of self-denial or self-punishment. This type of behavior often stems from feelings of guilt, which are, of course, a prevalent part of grief. This behavior may also stem from a vague cultural dictate that denies or disapproves of any type of self-indulgent behavior during the mourning period. The bereaved person is expected to mourn. To engage in frivolity is viewed as irreverent and disrespectful toward the deceased.

Diminished Sex Drive

Of all the effects on sexuality discussed in this chapter, the most commonly reported one is the decreased sex drive. It is a common problem and, in fact, quite normal, yet it can be one of the most personally disturbing outcomes for both husbands and wives. The following comments are from a young insurance salesman:

> After the usual waiting period, you would think that Donna and I would have been eager to resume our sexual activities, but it didn't happen that way. I simply had no interest in sex, not with her or anyone else. I really had a difficult time understanding this. At first I attributed it to work pressures, but even when we went on vacation, the usual sexual urges just weren't there. I began to question myself. I even did some things — movies, strip shows, and so forth — that usually "turned me on," but even they weren't interesting. It wasn't until several months later, when we began discussing another baby, that my sexual desires were revitalized.

Carolyn, a twenty-seven-year-old secretary, explained a similar reaction after delivering a stillborn son:

> I really felt sorry for Mike [her husband]. After the first few weeks, he was really ready for sex. For me, though, there was no interest. I went along, of course, but I can't say that I was responsive to him, nor did I enjoy it. I found myself using the "I'm tired" or "I don't feel well" excuses to avoid his overtures. It really had a negative impact on our marriage.

The sexual problems experienced by these two young people are not unusual. In fact, this type of reaction is to be expected after a loss. It is a common symptom of depression, an integral part of the grief process. Along with loss of appetite, fatigue, and insomnia, a decreased sex drive is characteristic of depressive reactions.

Other Effects

In addition to these five major negative effects on sexuality, there were two other rather specific effects that emerged in our interviews. The first relates to the husband's inclination to sex after stillbirth. The second concerns sexuality during the next pregnancy.

While it is difficult to project how common this reaction is, at least one husband experienced an ambivalent feeling toward intercourse after his wife delivered a stillborn infant. He explained his feelings this way:

> The first time we had sex after the baby died, I can remember I felt funny, very funny. It was like I was entering a place where a dead body had been. The sensuousness of it was gone. I think my wife felt the same way, but we never did really discuss it. I just remember that intercourse was very unappealing. In fact, I think it was repulsive. Thank heavens those feelings didn't last long.

Like so many other aspects of infant death and its effects on parents, this is a unique experience that is recognized as a problem only by those who have had to deal with it. While some couples experience immediate sexual difficulties, one mother suffered a "delayed" reaction. She became fearful of intercourse during a subsequent pregnancy. As she told us:

> Initially sex was better, much more intense; later, that changed. In the next pregnancy there was a great impact. I didn't want any [sexual activity] at all. I felt it might cause harm to the baby and I went totally in the opposite direction. I wanted him to stay away from me.

The extent to which these, and possibly other, effects are a part of the experience of grieving parents is still subject to further study. There are dimensions of sexuality and sexual dysfunction that appear to be characteristic of the majority of grieving parents, yet the individual intimacies and problems faced by specific couples may greatly vary.

Preventing Sexual Difficulties

While it is true that sexuality and sexual expressiveness is an ever-changing part of husband-wife relationships, we find that fetal/infant loss often brings abrupt changes. This most intimate part of marriage may suddenly be enriched, or it may quickly deteriorate. To the extent that couples use their sexual relationship as an expression of intimacy and affection, and as an extension of communication and mutual support, they will find an enhanced sex life is an unexpected outcome of their loss. On the other hand, if fear of, or obsession with, pregnancy, feelings of guilt, or personal inadequacy are manifested in the bedroom, the sexual relationship is sure to suffer.

For those couples who experience sexual difficulties, some of the following suggestions might be helpful:

1. Fear of pregnancy can be tempered through proper use of contraception. Elementary you say? Maybe so, yet many couples do not immediately resume contraceptive methods after the physician-imposed sexual "waiting period" is over.

2. Examine the basis of your fear of pregnancy. One loss does not mean that another loss is inevitable. Often your fears are very irrational.

3. If your fear of pregnancy and another loss becomes dysfunctional, seek genetic counseling. Often many of your questions can be answered and your fears overcome.

4. Give yourself time to grieve before attempting another pregnancy. Obsession with the idea of pregnancy is not synonymous with an honest desire to have a child. You cannot replace the baby you lost.

5. Don't allow sex to become mechanical. Sexuality is the most intimate method of self-expression and love. Likewise, a child should be the natural product of a loving relationship, not a mechanical sex

life. Be patient and allow yourself time. In most cases, the rewards of your effort will be realized.

6. Remember you are not alone. Other parents have lost infants, others have failed. Allowing your loss to lower your self-esteem may become a self-fulfilling prophecy. If you don't love yourself, how can others love you?

7. Don't punish yourself. You have lost your baby, but you need not forego the pleasures of life because of it. Try to get on top of the situation. Splurge a bit. Few people will ostracize you for it. Self-denial will not bring your baby back.

8. A decreased sex drive is a normal characteristic of depression. In time, as you resolve your grief, the old desires will return. Your loss has not rendered you physiologically frigid or impotent.

9. If you need professional help, get it. Sex therapy is a booming business today. Many couples are seeking help from trained professionals.

10. Change your environment. Take a vacation or check into a motel for a weekend. Do whatever is necessary to find or create an atmosphere that may be sexually stimulating for you and your mate.

Finally, and most importantly, remember that sex is a form of communication. As we have already seen, open channels of communication can prevent many problems and intervene in others. This is true of sexual problems as well. As a couple, you have experienced a tragic marital setback, but you're the same two people who conceived your lost child through your love for each other. There really is no rational reason for your loss to affect that love negatively.

MOTHERS, FRIENDS, AND FAMILY

Family and friends — those who supposedly care for you and love you the most — are often the cruelest in the things they say to you afterward. For instance: "You should be satisfied with the one healthy child you already have," or "Maybe the two of you should admit to yourselves that you aren't able to have another healthy baby." Then there are the friends who do finally call to ask how you are and end up trying to give you their medical history about the pregnancies they went through with their living children. You get very tired of hearing, "What are you so upset about?" "You're still young." "Oh, I'm sorry" — followed by a blank stare . . . and for me the real clincher — "What, you're going to try to have another? Why don't you leave well enough alone?"

—Judy

Once the mother returns home, she can expect the onset of expressions of sympathy. Family, friends, acquaintances, neighbors, and business associates will, through their honest sympathy or from the demands of social customs, have something to say to the bereaved mother. Too often, however, they do not engage in face to face communication, but rather they respond with sympathy cards. With the exception of closest family and friends (many times only family) the mother will find this to be a lonely period of mourning. It is difficult for a friend or even a relative to grieve for the death of a child they have never known. This lack of an established social circle around the infant can certainly account for the inability of most people to grieve with the mother for the child. For this reason, Americans have adopted the practice of sending sympathy cards as a symbolic acknowledgment of death. This is fortunate because the cards say to the mother that the sender recognizes the loss; it is unfortunate because the cards serve to isolate the mother, deny the importance of the death, and offer an easy way to avoid the grieving mother. As Charles Lippey, professor of religion at Clemson University has pointed out to us in personal conversation:

> The sympathy card offers a complex paradox. While it serves as a signal to acknowledge the reality of death, it simultaneously avoids direct discussion of death. It purports to communicate feeling, but masks lack of feeling or uncertainty over what feelings are socially appropriate. But it is in this paradox that the sympathy card derives its power and, accordingly, its wide currency in American society. The card allows the sender to acknowledge the death event while still preserving the taboo against talking about it explicitly. Acceptance and avoidance, nearness

and distance merge in the message of the word and in the act of sending it.

On one hand, a person may feel genuine sadness over the loss of a child, but either cannot find the words to express it or cannot face the reality of death. On the other hand, a person may not have particular feelings of sadness but may feel a sense of social obligation to acknowledge the death. The sympathy card can fulfill either need.

Sympathy cards directed to bereaved mothers can be divided into three basic types: (1) those sent by people who are simply meeting social obligations and that carry "standard messages"; (2) those that attempt expressions of feeling through standard messages but whose message is undermined by an inappropriate personal addition; and (3) those that do, in fact, convey sympathy through a sensitive, understanding, and personal message.

The first type consists of cards that are simply purchased, signed, and mailed. Generally this type of card is sent by either those who are simply meeting social obligations or by those who feel a sincere sympathy for the mother but cannot find adequate words to express their thoughts. Regardless of which category the sender is in, it is important that they consider the message contained in the card. Many times the message is so "commercialized" that little, if any, feeling is expressed.

> May this note of
> sympathy
> Help in some small way
> To bring you
> consolation
> And comfort
> you today.

> May God be near you

on this day
And bless you in
His precious way
And every sympathetic prayer
Ease your heart
And lessen care.

These two messages are so carefully rhymed that they approach vagueness. To many mothers they carry little feeling and serve only to increase feelings of frustration and loneliness.

Others carry more meaning. They are simple, to the point, and expressive:

May these
simple words
serve as an
expression
of our deepest
sympathy.

May it comfort you
to realize
That we understand
your loss.
Our sincerest
Sympathy is extended to you.

A second type of card commonly received by bereaved mothers is the standard commercial card on which the sender adds a personal note that is sometimes inappropriate to the situation and often detrimental to the mother's emotional condition. Consider the following sample:

Dear Susan:

I can't begin to tell you how sorry we were to learn of you losing your baby. We can understand and you have our sympathy. Although God took your baby before you hardly had him for your own, he so quickly made him an angel to intercede for you until you join him in heaven. Get well and strong and just hurry and have more babies.

Love,

While the intent of this note originally expressed sympathy, it was followed by the lack of acknowledgment that the baby was real — but rather just "an angel." Like the identical statement heard in the hospitals, this message evokes a feeling of "I don't want an angel, I want a baby." The note encourages the mother to "Hurry and have more babies," a piece of advice that is difficult for the mother, who is grieving her recent loss, to accept. A second, inappropriate offering is this:

Dear Jane:

We were very shocked tonight as we read in the paper about the tragedy which has just occurred in your family. I guess you must feel as though life has struck you a mighty blow — but you will soon get over it.

I not only invite you but I would like to request that you write soon — or when you feel up to it. I have always been interested in your friendship.

Sincerely,

The motivation behind a note like this is difficult to understand. The only response that could possibly be returned is, "Does it take losing my baby to make me important to you?"

The following three notes may be considered not only inappropriate, but also cruel.

Dear Kay,

We are sorry to hear about the baby. You are young and will have others.

Johnny is in bad shape. We have called the doctor. Was up with him several nights. His ulcer is giving him a hard time. He is in worse condition than when we were there. Sue has not had her baby yet, but is expecting it at any time.

Love,

Dear Karen,

We came back from our vacation Sunday night and learned of your loss. We are thinking of you and feeling for you. Life has many mysteries. Forget about this experience and think of the good things you have.

The mountains were so beautiful. We visited . . .

Sincerely,

Dear Sally,

It's hard to say in words how Jim and I felt when we heard about your baby. They say everything happens for the best, and God has a reason for them. It's hard sometimes to believe that way but we have to have faith that it is so.

Our Margaret was married Saturday and it was a beautiful wedding. Everything went so smoothly, weather and all, and she was a beautiful bride. We had a reception at the church and then about fifteen people stopped by the house. It broke up about three a.m. You worry and prepare for months, and it's all over in twenty minutes with two little words — "I do." Bye for now — write when you can.

As always,

These three notes are indicative of the way many people think about infant death. They feel that there has been no great loss to the mother; worse still, they feel little sorrow for the baby. Their trips, their worries, and their weddings are more important to them. Their insensitive messages can have devastating effects on the mother whose loss is real, who is searching for someone to share her grief, who may be asking herself, "Why me?" and who is feeling dejected and depressed. Such notes may long be remembered with bitterness and contempt.

The most effective communication during this period of time is a simple visit where face-to-face communication is possible. Great distances to travel, illness, and so forth may prevent such. In these cases, the third type of card can be a comforting communication to the mother.

This is a purchased card with a personal note added, or it may not even be a commercial card; it may be a personal letter. In either case, the message is thoughtful, expressive, and sensitive to the needs of the mother — not the sender. Consider the following examples:

Dear Susan,

Though I haven't seen you in quite some time, I join with many others in expressing my sincere sympathy in the loss of your son. I lost my first and only son in 1933 — and even the joy of our two daughters has never mitigated the loss. All I can say is that you never forget it, you just learn to live with it. This I'm sure you can do, though you will always say "Why, why did it have to happen to us?" You will also be surprised at the number of people who will tell you of their own losses that you had never known of before. So, my wish to you is that your love for each other will increase with your sorrow and that future years will add to your happiness.

Sincerely,

Dear Jan,

All words that I have are completely inadequate to express my feelings for you at this time of sorrow. Let it suffice for me to say that you are very much in my thoughts and I wish in all sincerity that there was something more I could do. I know you have probably spent much time asking why. Through your search for an answer I hope you find peaceful consolation. May the future bring the best to you. I am

Sincerely yours,

Dear Pam,

Little did I know yesterday when I saw you in the hospital what lay ahead for you. Let this be a simple assurance of sympathy and a prayer to and for you both, that through this tragedy and disappointment you will find strength and comfort. Perhaps in the future you will find the dream fulfilled that you longed for this time.

Sincerely,

Dear Jo,

I have just returned from a trip and was so distressed to learn of the death of your baby. I just wanted you to know you have my prayers, and to say I'm sorry I could not be with you in your time of sorrow. If there is anything I can do for you please let me know.

Sincerely,

The positive messages such cards can convey are numerous — the acknowledgement of death and recognition of loss, the honest feelings and offers of help. The mother is not admonished to forget or "to have more babies." In general, the expressions are supportive of the mother's needs rather than directed to the needs of the sender.

These samples may be useful as models for those people who find words difficult to express but who feel compelled to say something. Sympathy cards can and do serve their purposes, but only if they are directed to the mother and are truly sensitive to her needs.

While some people find it difficult to engage in face-to-face communication during this time, others (usually relatives and close friends) will visit the home to express sympathy or to help the mother with household duties during her convalescence. Often bereaved mothers find this support beneficial. A secondary effect of this support is the strengthening effect it has on relationships.

Sometimes, however, through inappropriate communication or a lack of understanding of the mourning process, problems can arise. One young mother expressed her frustrations as follows:

> There are times when you just want to kill people for what they say to you, people who are trying to help but are not helping. For instance, I have a very dear friend who asked me to go out to lunch with her shortly after the baby died; but the only thing she wouldn't talk about was the baby, and that was the only thing I wanted to talk about. I really felt a need to talk. She wouldn't let me. This pretty much held true for all my friends — they didn't want to upset me, and I realized that if I talked, it upset them. They weren't ready for it. I didn't want them to think I was a basket case, so I gradually pulled away. Little do they know how much it hurt.

The bereaved mother must be allowed to talk about her experience. The best friend she can have is an empathetic listener. Too often, however, during the initial period of grief when people are receptive to listening, the mother, still depressed and in a state of shock, is unable to talk. However, once the physical recuperation has been completed and the reality of the loss sinks in, the situation reverses itself. The mother then experiences an intense need to talk. Unfortunately, friends, relatives, and acquaintances have already paid their respects for an infant they did not know and they are now ready to forget. As one woman explained:

> Well, the crying I tried to keep to myself. I felt like I had to put up the pretense that I was over it, because I didn't want them to feel bad. The only way I can explain it is that it was a lonely grief. You had to wait until no one was around before you could cry. If you didn't, you'd have everyone acting like "For crying out loud, it could have been a lot worse; at least you're fine." I even think my husband felt that way.

The mother, therefore, finds herself in an extremely undesirable situation. She wants to talk, but now there is no one to listen. She suffers intense grief, but in virtual isolation. Even her husband cannot comprehend these delayed, intense feelings. The short-lived compassion of friends and relatives turns to "get over this thing," "put it behind you," "don't dwell on it." They feel she has grieved enough. After all, the child was really unknown (and many times unnamed), and certainly she can have others. It is difficult for them to understand the depth of feeling the mother has for the dead child; as a result, support is withdrawn when it is needed the most. Communication channels are closed and a rigid and cruel isolation is imposed on the mother. To her, there appears to be no escape. She represses her feeling; her grief remains unresolved.

Such is the social atmosphere into which the mother must reintegrate herself. She needs to talk, but no one wants to listen. She feels guilty in bringing up the topic but is many times faced with "How's your baby?" from an unknowing acquaintance, and she feels self-conscious, conspicuous, and lonely. Excerpts from our interviews illustrate the problem these women face:

> I didn't at first feel any more self-conscious than I usually am, but then there were some horrendous experiences. Like, one of my mother's

friends rushed up to me and said, "Oh, you had your baby! What did you have?" I replied "A girl, but she died." I wanted to cut her tongue out, and I didn't know whether I felt worse for myself or her. That made me very hesitant to go out with people who knew I had been pregnant.

My stomach did not go down immediately, and I guess I looked pregnant. I was very reluctant to go out among people. I had a very horrible experience with one woman I had never met before. She asked me when my baby was due. My first thought was, this woman's going to die when she hears that not only has my baby been born, but has also died. So I tried to get it all out in one breath. She looked at my stomach, said "Had the baby?" and it went from bad to worse. She never acknowledged the loss.

We must realize that, even after the mother begins to reestablish her social life, she has not forgotten and probably still feels a need to talk. And she may be afraid to mention her loss for fear of making others uncomfortable. It is important to let her know that it is perfectly all right to talk, that you are willing to listen, and that you are supportive of her. Lasting friendships can be established or destroyed through appropriate or inappropriate communication.

Here are some DOs and DON'Ts for communicating with bereaved parents as suggested by The Bereaved Parent's Group of Winston-Salem, North Carolina:

DOs

1. Do say you are sorry about their pain and what happened to their child.

2. Do allow them to express the grief they are feeling.

3. Do allow them to talk as much as they want about the child they lost.

4. Do give special attention to the child's brothers and sisters, both at the funeral and in the months to come. They, too, are hurt and confused and in need of attention — which their parents may not be

able to give them.

5. Do reassure the parents that they did everything they could, that the medical care their child received was the best, or whatever else you know to be true and positive.

DON'Ts

1. Don't avoid the bereaved because you are uncomfortable. Being avoided adds pain to an already intolerable experience.

2. Don't say, "You ought to be feeling better by now," or anything that implies a judgment about their feelings.

3. Don't avoid mentioning the child's name for fear of reminding them of their loss. They haven't forgotten it!

4. Don't say, "You can always have another child." Even if they wanted to and could, another child would not replace the child they lost.

5. Don't make comments that suggest the care in the emergency room, hospital, or wherever was inadequate. Parents are always plagued by feelings of doubt and guilt. Family and friends should be careful not to sow seeds of doubt.

Mothers, Doctors, And Hospitals

DOCTORS

Few professionals receive more respect from the general public than do physicians. Their high status is due, in part, to society's expectations and concern with good health and the ability of doctors to maintain it. Unfortunately, the public often has expectations concerning the quality of their performance that fail to account for their human frailties. Such frailties often appear when the physician is involved in a death-related experience. We believe that mothers and fathers need to be aware of the dilemmas faced by physicians as they encounter and experience death in their practices. We all need to be mindful that our doctors are human beings complete with the weaknesses of other human beings. In spite of our expectations, they are not as omnipotent as we would like them to be. Although we have every right to expect them to deal with our losses in a highly sensitive and understanding manner, we need to be prepared for disappointments. And the disappointments and misunderstandings that occur are often most noticeable in relationships involving mothers who have just lost babies.

Family physicians and specialists responsible for the care of these mothers often fail to understand the significance of their loss; consequently, they respond to them in ways that are, at best, less than satisfactory. The relationships between these mothers and their doctors (represented almost exclusively by the obstetrical and pediatric specialties) are often fraught with conflict and difficulty, not in regard to the medical care received, but rather to the inept management of the circumstances surrounding the death of the infant. The problems, more often than not, stem from poor communication. The mother often perceives the physician as being insensitive, aloof, and unconcerned. For example, Martha, a twenty-four-year-old expectant mother, told of her experience:

I was taken to the emergency room after I miscarried and the doctor and

117

the nurse were working on me and he asked for a pan. I had no idea what was going on, only that I was bleeding very badly. Then all of a sudden the doctor held up for me to see, a mass of flesh about four or five inches long and an inch or two wide, all bloody and dripping, and said rather dryly, "Well, there's your baby, lady; you lost it." I still can't talk to anyone about this and it happened over two years ago.

This experience may not be typical, but it is one of a variety of physician responses that indicates insensitivity and general misperception of the significance of perinatal death to the mother.

The difficulty that physicians have in accepting fetal/infant death as a genuine tragedy for the family may stem from their fears and attitudes toward death in general and from training that orients them toward life. In a study of attitudes toward death, Herman Feifel found that even though physicians thought less about death than did control-group subjects (patients and other nonprofessionals), they were more afraid of death. He suggested that some physicians may enter medicine to govern their own above-average fears of death.[1] These attitudes may be characteristic of their personalities, but they also may be shaped by their medical training as well.

Training helps physicians transform their personal fear of death in general into a "neutral" professional attitude toward the death of the patient. Young physicians, for example, in their early years of training have little contact with the realities of death and dying. David and Laurel Rabin describe the medical student's first professional encounter with the dead human body in the first-year anatomy course.[2] They point out that the student is not really bothered by the fact that the cadavers were once living human beings with names and pasts. To the medical students, cadavers have no pasts — no names. They are simply objects from which one can learn.

In the second year students take their first courses in pathology and usually attend their first autopsy. The autopsy is a very unique experience because students encounter, perhaps for the first time, the body of a person they consider to be real, as opposed to "just a cadaver." The students also have access to the complete medical history of the person up to the time of death. In this encounter, students often find they cannot hold the same attitude toward this victim as they did toward the first-year cadaver; they now associate the corpse with a living person. Rabin and Rabin note that it is this first autopsy that makes the student "painfully aware of the awesome responsibility the physician accepts and of the human limitations that constrain even the most skilled" (p. 173).

Thus the autopsy room teaches students the vulnerability of the medical profession to death. The pathologist does not always have all the answers concerning causes of death, nor is the physician's diagnosis always right. Students realize that, although death can sometimes be postponed for prolonged periods, death in the end always emerges the victor, sometimes sooner than anticipated.

In their last two years of training, medical students participate in clinical experiences. Implicit throughout their medical training, however, is the idea that death means failure, either of the physician or of medicine as a whole. Thus, young doctors enter the field of medicine armed not only with the latest techniques that medicine can devise, but also with an attitude — a product of their training — that because it is within their power to keep patients alive, it is their responsibility to do so. To do less would be to admit failure.

Consequently, impending death becomes something to work against, to avoid at any cost. When death does occur, it is considered the result of medical accident or technical error. The physician may not only be unprepared to accept it, but also may not know how to accept it. What to do when the event occurs — that seems to be the crux of the problem, particularly in cases of perinatal death.

Upon completing their education, approximately eighty-five percent of all medical students enter a specialty. This is an important factor in understanding the interaction patterns that emerge in physician-family relationships after death occurs. Rabin and Rabin have indicated that the specialty a young physician chooses dictates, to a large degree, future experience with death: "Many students enter specialties that provide primary care — obstetrics, pediatrics, and internal medicine — where death is not a common occurrence. When it does occur, it can be a profoundly disturbing event" (p. 175). Young pediatricians and obstetricians find it difficult to relate humanely to death and dying, not because they have no feelings or suffer no grief, but because their training and professional attitudes do not permit them to deal effectively with death on a personal level. At times, they do not really know what to do when the event occurs; consequently, they do nothing.

According to George Gilson, the obstetrician who "loses" a baby at birth will in many cases go through a mourning-separation process for the infant in the same way that parents do, though not necessarily with the same degree of intensity. The doctor, too, looks upon that birth with an anticipated sense of joy, but suddenly finds the need to deal with a tragedy. Medical training simply does not prepare the obstetrician to deal openly with death on such a personal level. As a consequence, at this time the doctor may be unable to provide the support that the family needs and must have. This lack of support may stem from the doctor's own sense of inadequacy, or feelings of failure and helplessness, and perhaps even a sense of responsibility for the death.[3] The pediatrician experiences similar reactions in a comparable situation. The pediatrician, too, is oriented to life, and death produces a high degree of anxiety.

The way the physician responds and displays feelings certainly will have an impact upon how the mother handles her loss. The situation is often compounded by the reactions of the mother toward the doctor. As she passes through the stage of volatile emotions, anger erupts, anger that is often targeted at the doctor.

This reaction of the mother only intensifies the psychological hurt the physician may already be feeling. Protective defenses then come into play, and consequently the doctor may avoid the grieving mother and father.

The majority of mothers we interviewed indicated that the relationships between themselves and their physicians were usually altered and sometimes terminated after their loss. Frequently, the mothers indicated that obstetricians showed no willingness to counsel them; nor did they display much concern after the death.

Marlene, the mother of a stillborn girl, told us of her experience with the obstetrician:

> He avoided me like the plague . . . . He even avoided my husband. When Steve finally did corner him, all he said was "these things happen" and "we should try to put it behind us." He really offered no support at all other than a few statements about what he thought the problem was . . . . He had about as much compassion as a stone.

Nancy, also the mother of a stillborn girl, had the following to say about her relationship with her obstetrician:

> I had a fairly good relationship with him during my prenatal care. I thought he was friendly and caring. Apparently, delivering that dead baby really shook him up . . . . He appeared so distant and could hardly look me in the eye . . . . I needed his support and assurance so badly, but he just disappeared into the woodwork.

Some obstetricians feel their job is done once the child has been delivered, and that the burden of counseling the bereaved is someone else's responsibility.

Pediatricians can find themselves in a comparable situation. When a baby is born with serious complications, the obstetrician usually steps aside and the pediatrician takes over. If the infant should die, consoling the mother should then become the physician's responsibility. Yet some pediatricians believe that thrusting a bereaved mother upon them, after the death of an infant who was so badly malformed or diseased that there was little chance of saving it, is an unfair tactic, particularly when they do not know the family or the child. They claim that they cannot afford to spend their time counseling parents when other sick children are waiting. Under these circumstances, both pediatrician and obstetrician turn away, leaving the mother and father to deal with their loss alone, leaving them the victims of the highly specialized medicine that might have saved their child. The following interview excerpt relates how one mother felt about her relationship with her pediatrician:

> The doctor just really didn't give a damn about us! Christopher lived five days under his care and you would have expected some show of feeling when he died, but the doctor simply went about his business just as if nothing had happened. Maybe it was his way of covering his feelings . . . . But, my God, he should have known that we had feelings too!

Often the attempts made by obstetricians or pediatricians to deal with grieving parents are strained and filled with tensions. Such expressions as "Forget about this," "You're young enough to have another child," "You should be happy that the baby was normal and well-developed," or "You now have a little angel in heaven," are all examples of inappropriate things said to parents who have experienced a loss. Such expressions are neither what parents need nor want to hear at these critical times. They sound callous and show a profound lack of understanding.

This problem of communication is due in part to a lack of understanding of the role requirements by both doctors and parents. Doctors face a real dilemma; they are expected to be healers, but when they and/or their remedies fail and death occurs, they are expected to become counselors, friends, and consolers. This role switch is difficult for some physicians, impossible for others. In some cases, personal fears and attitudes about death will cause the physician to display insensitive behavior, to react inappropriately, to say things that do not fit the situation, or to give personal advice that is ill-founded. This is not intentional, of course, but such responses and actions, colored more by emotions than by professional objectivity, can alienate or anger the parents. The physician responds to human tragedy like any other human being — with common emotional responses such as guilt, anger, resentment, and a sense of failure. Sometimes the physician deals with these uncomfortable feelings by avoiding contact with the parents and, in so doing, gives an impression of indifference and insensitivity. Under these circumstances, conflicts can occur. It may be the parents who do not understand that such reactions are "normal" human responses. Unfortunately, the parents are also the ones who will suffer the consequences.

In other cases, the physician's discomfort in the presence of death may preclude any kind of response, causing, instead, withdrawal behind the facade of professional objectivity, leaving the parents to face the bewilderment of death without guidance or consolation. Again, it may be the parents who do not understand his reaction and who, regrettably, suffer the consequences.

The responsibility for success in relationships between parents and physicians at these critical times falls on the physician, not the parents. It is the physician who should strive to improve the quality of the interaction. The physician must shed anxieties about death and misconceptions about the significance of infant death to assume the dual role of counselor and consoler to the family.

We do not mean to leave the impression that all physicians respond to the death of a fetus or newborn indifferently or insensitively. A recent trend in medical training emphasizes total patient care. It stresses the importance of the psychological and social aspects of illness and their bearing on diagnosis and prognosis. Because of the influence of these newer training programs, as well as individual personalities and experiences in dealing with loss and reaction to loss, some physicians have become adept in dealing with parents who lose infants. These physicians are very sensitive to the need for counseling and consoling. Following are two excerpts that illustrate the appreciation mothers have for physicians who approach the situation with sensitivity:

Dr. _____ was a marvelous man. I'll never forget him as long as I live. He came into my room that night and sat on the edge of my bed; tears were running down his cheeks . . . . He said they couldn't save him, that Stephen had died . . . . He just sat there holding my hand . . . . I guess you could say we cried together . . . . He came in every day, at least twice . . . . We talked and talked and talked . . . . He went over and over all the details of what they did and how he died for both my husband and me, until I had it straight and had no more questions. Several days after I returned home he called me and I guess we talked for about an hour. He just wanted to know how I was doing and if I had any more questions . . . . He was a wonderful man.

Another mother told us:

It was the neonatologist who took over Michael's case after he was transferred to Children's Hospital who I remember most. That man was a saint! He anticipated our every need. Michael was there about fifteen days before he died and we visited him constantly . . . . I spent several nights there and Dr. _____ would come in and sit down and spend considerable time with us, detailing what he was doing and how Michael was progressing. He was very honest, and told us that his chances of making it were slim . . . . He was very concerned with how we were doing . . . . We came to depend upon him totally . . . . We felt that in this big impersonal hospital, here was one person we could really count on. When Michael died, he was absolutely wonderful . . . . As busy as he was, he took the time out to attend Michael's funeral . . . . He was such a sensitive man.

Many physicians have come to believe that they must not become "involved," but must maintain their professional objectivity in all cases and under all circumstances. This is nonsense.

The physician who responds to the tragedy of loss as a human being is no less of a physician. Responding to the total needs of parents who suffer losses requires an understanding and compassionate attitude. Physicians who can express emotion, who can grieve over the loss of an infant along with the parents, are often remembered for their sensitivity and compassion. As one mother told us:

> As I said earlier, I delivered a stillborn boy. I'll never forget the scene in the delivery room. It was as much a surprise to the doctor as it was to me. I remember the doctor got very somber looking — that was the first instant that I knew something was wrong. The nurses were crying. He came to my side, bent down, put his arm over my stomach and said with great compassion in his voice that the baby was dead. I could see the tears in his eyes. He asked me if I wanted to see the baby and I said yes. He went over and brought the baby, wrapped in a blanket, and placed it in my arms. He told me that as far as he could tell, the baby was perfectly normal. He died of cord strangulation. All the while, Dr. _____ was standing by my side holding my hand tightly. There was a genuine "atmosphere of grief" in that room. I can't explain it but it helped me deal with this thing. I thought, this man is grieving for my baby. My baby was that important! It was not just my loss, but his, too. This is how I remember Dr. _____ ; this is how I will always remember him.

Good physicians will come to realize that there is no such thing as a deathless specialty, and that to be effective in their profession, they must train themselves to deal with death on a personal level.

To parents who experience the loss, dying is not a simple biological process to be understood as a failure of medical technology. Rather, it involves real people — even when these people are unborn fetuses. Death disrupts significant relationships and severs family bonds. When fetal or infant death occurs, parents have many needs. The physician can best fill these needs by supplying the parents with information about the causes and circumstances of the death, and by being sensitive to their emotional state during the initial phase of the grieving process.

Parents, especially the mothers, are often riddled with guilt when their infant dies. The physician is the only person who can supply the kind of information necessary to relieve the guilt. It is natural to want to know why, how, and what went wrong. There is nothing more helpful than a physician who is available, giving comfort and support, conveying information in a compassionate and understanding manner, and telling the parents how their loss might affect them in the weeks and months to come.

Postvention is the name Edwin Shneidman has given to those appropriate and helpful acts done to reduce the traumatic impact of grief.[4] Like disease, grief can take a heavy toll, but it can be treated and controlled. Alfred Herzog has outlined three stages of postvention: resuscitation — working with the patient who is trying to cope with the initial shock of grief in the first twenty-four hours; rehabilitation — consultation with family members from the first to the sixth month; and renewal — the healthy tapering off of the mourning process from six months on.[5]

The physician's role as counselor and consoler is obviously limited by circumstances and need. For simple pragmatic reasons, it cannot extend through the entire postvention period. The physician's primary responsibility to the family should be assumed during the resuscitation stage. This is a critical period in the lives of the parents. It is during this stage that the physician shoulders the greatest responsibility in managing the death and responding to the family's needs. What is said and done during this period will leave a lasting imprint.

What can be done to improve the relationship between physician and parents during this critical time? C. Everett Koop, in an article about supporting the family in cases of chronic illness, gives a number of suggestions that we have adapted and expanded to fit the circumstances surrounding the loss of an infant.[6]

These suggestions all pertain to the immediate situation and are designed as a form of crisis-intervention counseling to take place within the first twenty-four to forty-eight hours. Parents need to be aware of how these suggestions can function to relieve them of some of the trauma of the loss they are experiencing.

When the time comes for the physician to talk with the family about what has happened (miscarriage or stillbirth) or what is about to happen (premature or birth trauma where death is probable), consideration of the following points will greatly enhance the physician's effectiveness:

1. The news should be given to the family in the best possible physical surroundings, such as a room specifically for that purpose, or in the privacy of the mother's hospital room. It should not be given in the ward, in the corridor, in the lobby of the hospital, or any place where the parents cannot express emotion without embarrassment. This rule should be observed in all cases.

2. At the time the news is given, both parents should be together. In the case of a stillbirth, the father may be the first to know but he should be with the mother when she is told. If grandparents and others are present, it must be made certain they will provide stability and support. Preferably, however, the parents should be the first to know.

3. According to Koop, the actual wording of the announcement of death or impending death should be "gentle rather than abrupt, compassionate while factual, and free of scientific terms that are not understood as well as free of double talk that will leave the family uncertain and permit the physician to escape to more pleasant tasks" (p. 190). In addition, the announcement should come directly from the primary physician. Parents should not be subjected to cliches and thoughtless statements such as "you will get over it," or "it's not the end of the world," or "you're young enough to have another."

4. If the infant is born alive, but there is good reason to

believe that death is imminent, the physician should explain to the parents in simple terms exactly what the problem is or what he perceives it to be. Later, after the initial impact, the physician can describe for the parents the steps that will be taken to deal with the problem. No matter what the prognosis, however, hope should be maintained and assurances given that no matter what the outcome, everything possible will be done to support the infant. Satisfying the requirements of this step demands a series of frequent contacts between parents and physician. Parents have numerous questions that can be answered only through repeated interaction with their physician.

5. The physician should remember that some people hear only what they want to hear. If the parents are screening out unpleasant information, it may be necessary to bring in another member of the family or a very close friend to help interpret the unpleasant facts.

6. A kindly gesture, such as an arm around the father, holding the hands of both parents, or even the ability to shed tears may seem embarrassing to the physician, but such responses are frequently remembered later as outstanding acts of moral support.

Although we must recognize the importance of the role of physician as counselor and consoler during the initial stages of grief, subsequent postvention activities can be performed by others in the community who are close to the family and who can understand and empathize with them. Such individuals can be friends, close relatives, or neighbors who are not directly and intimately involved in the trauma. It is often difficult, if not impossible, however, for families to find individuals who can function as sympathetic listeners and upon whom they can depend for support when the physician's initial role has been completed.

In some communities, individuals who have suffered similar kinds of losses have formed voluntary organizations whose purpose is to help pull the families through the difficult postvention stages. Members of these organizations are trained as "therapeutic listeners," whose function is to give solace and comfort to families who cannot find it elsewhere.

In communities where such voluntary organizations do not exist, specially trained public health nurses can often perform a similar function by providing needed information and counseling during the rehabilitation period. Every community needs some group or organization to pick up where the doctor leaves off.

Obstetricians and pediatricians can take the lead in communicating to appropriate agencies and organizations the need for rehabilitative counseling and consolation for families and parents who have suffered the tragedy of infant death. The training required is not elaborate; it involves selecting individuals who are warm, supportive, and compassionate, who have an ability to listen, and who can develop an understanding of normal grief reactions. Such an effort may take time, but the rewards for the community and, more particularly, for the family will be great.

The "renewal" phase of the postvention period is more difficult to deal with because during this period, which begins about six months after the death, parents are virtually unable to find sympathetic listeners. The period of crisis has ended; the questions have been answered; the agony and the anguish have passed. The need still remains, however, to express many of the subtle feelings that linger beneath the surface. Many times these feelings will be the sadness that comes from remembering all the little details that surrounded the loss. A need simply to talk often remains.

The physician can perform an invaluable service at this point in postvention. An office visit for the mother, or, preferably, for both parents, can be arranged about six months into the postvention period. In fact, parents should initiate these visits if doctors do not suggest them themselves. The physician's function at this time should be simply to listen and offer assurances that the feelings and reactions that the parents pour out are normal. Parents should have additional opportunities to ask other questions that may have occurred to them during the six-month interval. Incidentally, parents who have experienced this kind of thoughtful intervention, initiated by the physician, always remember them with great affection and appreciation.

By talking about feelings, parents find that their hurt becomes more bearable, and the sadness gradually dissipates. As long as these feelings exist — sometimes for months or years — there will be a need to express them. Professionals — doctors, nurses, hospital attendants, social workers — who are involved in the events surrounding perinatal death can contribute to the resolution of the parents' grief only when they recognize that there is no limit to the consolation they can offer.

HOSPITALS

When I asked to see the twins, both my husband and the nurse said "No." But I knew that I could not let them go without seeing them. I finally got to see them, but not to touch them. I never got to say goodbye. Three days down the road I knew this was a mistake.

—Michelle

You suffer doubts, misgivings, and the most horrible of all — guilt. I suffered tremendously. I asked to see my son and was refused. I was kept on the maternity floor where I went through agony listening to new babies cry. The cold treatment I received from the hospital personnel was dreadful. They evidently thought it was better to avoid me than answer my questions. The doctor never spoke to me of my baby again. It was as though he never existed.

—Gloria

Members of the hospital staff, particularly emergency room and maternity floor personnel, are usually the first people to encounter the mother who is experiencing excessive bleeding, whose baby has stopped moving, or who is faced with the realiza-

tion that her infant has died. The manner in which they deal with
her can have a great impact on her future well-being. Each type of
loss (i.e., stillbirth, spontaneous abortion, neonatal death, and
SIDS) presents the staff with special problems, and each should be
handled differently. Throughout our interviews, we were shocked
at the problems mothers encountered during their hospital stays.
Most of them could have been avoided with sincere concern and
appropriate communication.

The first type we will look at is stillbirth. One mother had this
to say:

> My first thoughts were that it couldn't be true. I was awake during the
> entire delivery. I wasn't sure what was going on. In fact, I kept fainting
> and accusing them of sneaking in some anesthesia. The first time I
> realized I was in trouble was when the doctor told them to prepare for an
> emergency Caesarean. I delivered before they did that and from the dead
> silence, and my baby not crying, I knew.

The nurse in the antepartum clinic may be the first person to
encounter a mother who is concerned about the well-being of her
baby. In most cases the mother's hospital visit is prompted by a lack of
movement of the child. During the initial examination, her fears about
the child's life may be confirmed, but few mothers immediately
accept the inevitable; they cling to the hope that a mistake has been
made, that the baby is sleeping, or that the exam will resuscitate him.
This is a difficult period for the mother. She fluctuates between denial
and acceptance that she is, in fact, carrying a dead child. Many
thoughts may haunt her: "How morbid! I am carrying a dead child!"
"Is there anything I can do to revive my baby?" "Why did this happen
to me?" "Maybe everything will be all right." "When will labor
begin?" "What will my husband say?" The following comment is
illustrative of this confusion:

> I asked him [the OB] what the chances were for the baby. He said fifty-

fifty, which is what I expected. Even though I knew it was chancy and that I would probably lose the child, I was still hoping, because I was born at seven months, too. I kept thinking if I could make it, my baby can make it. But I was terribly upset and terribly nervous at the same time. I didn't want my husband to know because he would be so upset. I guess, really, I knew the baby was lost.

During this time hospital personnel can best serve the mother simply by listening. It is important that they not build false hopes by such expressions as "Everything will turn out O.K.," or "There's always the chance that a mistake has been made." Such statements only facilitate denial and complicate the mother's confusion. It is also inadvisable to recount other similar experiences to the mother, such as "This same thing happened to a friend of mine a few years ago and she . . ." or "We had a woman here last month who . . .," and so forth. For this mother, she is all that counts; it is her baby, and the time is now. More than anything, she needs reassurance that her feelings of helplessness, failure, confusion, and depression are normal. A sensitive, nonjudgmental ear, a friend who understands and allows her tears, and a companion to avert the loneliness are the needs of the mother at this point. For until delivery, she will alternate between denial and acceptance of reality.

Labor becomes a stressful time for both mother and staff. The mother anticipating a stillbirth is filled, not with happy anticipation, but with hours of fruitless labor from which she will derive only relief, not reward. The staff faces the awkward and uncomfortable task of trying to make it as easy as possible for her. All the normal fears and anxieties of labor and delivery are heightened.

During this phase, the mother and her feelings must be acknowledged. Unlike the initial antepartum stage, where simple listening was adequate and silence golden, a lack of response or silence may now be interpreted as a lack of concern. Simple statements like, "I know this is difficult for you," or "I'm here, I

understand your problem, and I feel for you," can relax the tension
of the moment. Again, it is extremely important to listen to the
mother, to hear what she says, to respond appropriately, and to
avoid the creation of false hopes. For this mother, everything is not
"O.K." Consequently, statements to the contrary may appear
callous and show a definite lack of understanding.

In the delivery room, the inevitable encounter with the reality
of death occurs. Tension abounds as the physicians and nurses
deliver a stillborn infant rather than a living child, and death
becomes undeniable. For many mothers recovering from sedation,
a simple "I'm sorry," or the silence of nonverbal sadness answers
her one pressing question: "Is my baby dead?"

At this point a severe break in communication often occurs
between the hospital staff and the mother, a break that may have
disastrous effects. Unable to find words of comfort, the staff will
often involve itself with perfunctory tasks of physical care, view-
ing the mother as simply another patient with physical needs to be
met and ignoring her emotional needs. As one woman expressed it:

> No one spoke to me about the baby. We wanted a natural childbirth to
> really experience the true closeness of mother, father, and child, and the
> joy of hearing the first cries and just plain feeling that I, not the doctor,
> was giving birth. When the cry did not come, I was just whisked away,
> like the moment never existed. It is a deep pain that I'll never forget.

Through appropriate verbal and nonverbal communication, the
few minutes immediately following the confirmation of stillbirth can
be used to best advantage by encouraging the mother to express her
feelings and begin the grieving process, rather than attempting to
delay the reaction through sedation, as is often the case.

The nature and consequences of such an approach were
expressed by one woman as follows:

> One of the nurses, one that I thought was very good, asked me why I was

133

> crying. I said, "My baby has died!" She responded, "Well, you can have
> another baby. Your parents and husband are waiting for you. Keep a stiff
> upper lip, I don't want to see any crying." Right away they're telling you
> not to grieve. I should have given her a stiff upper lip . . . but, you know,
> you do anything they say. Then they put me under sedation.

Statements such as "It's all right to cry," or "Words are difficult at
a time like this, but we feel your loss and understand how painful it
is for you," will open the door for an outpouring of emotion.

During this highly emotional period, many future uncertain-
ties may be avoided if the mother is able to see or hold her baby. In
fact, many mothers harbor an intense desire to be able just once to
see and hold the child. It is tragic if this need remains unfulfilled
simply because the mother is unaware that she has this option. In
many hospitals, standard procedures do not allow it. In those
hospitals where it is permitted, the ritual of the delivery room,
either intentionally or unintentionally, often takes priority.

By seeing and/or touching the baby, many mothers are better
able to cope with their grief, because their ability to express grief
becomes rooted in reality. The loss becomes real; denial is no
longer possible. Seeing the baby also gives it an identity. Details of
weight, hair color, and other characteristics will never have to be
wondered about. The willingness on the part of the staff to allow
the mother to see her baby represents an important consideration,
one she will remember for years.

Seeing the baby also relieves the fears of possible malformation and imperfection, fears that sometimes plague mothers who
do not have this option. This point is very evident when we
compare the following experiences. One mother commented:

> Our son was the second of the twins [we lost] and was born with a hairlip
> and cleft palate, two defects his sister did not have. It was immediately
> apparent at birth but it was not nearly as frightening seeing it as it would
> have been if I had only been told. I'm sure my imagination would have
> played many tricks.

Another offered this comment:

> My three daughters who died were all alive at birth and lived from two
> hours to three days. They died from extreme prematurity — ten to twelve
> weeks. I was completely awake at their births, heard them cry, saw them,
> and even held one. They were beautiful, perfectly formed, and incredi-
> bly small (12 inches, 1 pound 10 ounces); but most of all, they were mine
> — conceived, wanted, and loved by my husband and me.

The hospital staff should realize that the object of their concern is
the mother rather than their own personal fears or values. The
choice to see and/or hold the baby should be the mother's decision
alone and the decision should be respected and supported.

Rationalizing that they are protecting the parents, the staff
may simply be denying their own fears of death. Such evasions or
deceptions can leave the mother with unnecessary fears and anxieties about the appearance of her child. If there is a problem of
malformation, a sensitive but straightforward verbal preparation
for what she will see, and a strategically placed blanket, is, for the
most part, all that is necessary. A mother will accept a malformed
child if she is prepared for it. This is a better approach than
allowing the mother to suffer from the fantasy that she had carried a
severely deformed child. Put simply, if the mother chooses to see
her baby, the facts should be given to her regarding development,
skin color, etc. "He is a perfect child, but he will be somewhat
discolored and still. He has blue eyes and blond hair like you."
"Don't be afraid to cry; she is a baby worth crying about." As with
most life situations, the positive will be remembered and the
negative forgotten. If the mother's need for seeing and touching are
met, the benefits will far outweigh the hurt and many questions
will be answered.

When the mother is returned to the maternity ward, she will
again feel the pain of grief. Reunited with family and friends, she
will hear many comments and face uncomfortable situations that

will have an emotional impact on her. Good communication is vital during this postpartum period. Expression of grief at this time is usually characterized by depression, anger, guilt, and a sense of failure. There may be long periods of crying and other forms of overt emotion. During this phase the mother should be encouraged to talk about her experience. Too many times, however, she is discouraged from doing so by such comments as "You're fine now, let's see how soon we can get you home," or "Don't think about the baby, let's take care of you." Such comments serve only to block the mother's need to relive the details of her experience.

This is a time when interstaff communication is essential for hospital personnel. The entire staff should be informed of the death of the baby. Many mothers who have lost a child harbor very strong feelings about seeing other babies. This is, in part, a defense; nevertheless, it is a very real feeling and one that by all means should be recognized. This is not the time to force other children on the mother in hopes that it will help her, temporarily, to forget her loss. It can be cruel and unjust to return a mother who has just lost her baby to the maternity ward. Hospital policy and procedure should be flexible enough to place her on another ward away from new mothers and crying babies. If she is moved to another part of the hospital, the staff who have contact with her should be briefed concerning her loss. This applies not only to the professional staff but also to aides, volunteers, and others who may have contact with her. A failure to do this may lead to very unfortunate events, as illustrated by these comments:

> A nurse who didn't know the baby had died kept coming in and nagging me about getting up to go to the bathroom and kept asking me things like, "How much does your baby weigh?" and things like that. I finally told her the baby died and she disappeared! I guess I scared her, but it made me so angry that she didn't know.

And these:

They moved me from the OB floor to keep me from hearing the crying babies or seeing them brought to the rooms, but you never know where you will be put — maybe in orthopedics or somewhere like that. Every nurse would come in and say, "What are you here for?" or something like that. They wouldn't know why you were there. And then when you would tell them, they couldn't wait to get out of the room. I ended up with an infection because I couldn't take a Sitz bath. The nurses seemed to be unaware of my problem.

And finally:

Even though I was in a private room, this was probably one of the hardest times I had. When the pediatricians made their rounds, all I could hear next door, in the hallway, everywhere, was "Mrs. Jones, your big eight-pound baby boy is ready to go home," or "Very good, we drank eight ounces of formula today." That got to me. But, the clincher came when they brought me another mother's baby to nurse . . . by mistake!

Events such as these could be avoided by some simple procedures such as placing a symbol on the mother's chart and on the door of her room. This could inform all personnel that this mother has lost a child, handle with care.

While staff involvement with the mother diminishes as she approaches dismissal, her emotional condition should remain a primary concern in spite of her improved physical condition. The mother's fragile emotional state should be respected by everyone until she has left the hospital. As one mother told us:

Everything seemed to have been going as smoothly as possible, considering the circumstances. Most of the nurses knew what my situation was and treated me accordingly. It wasn't until I was ready to go home that something really bad happened. My husband had gone to pick up the car and a nurse was helping get my things together. They had wheeled me all the way down to the elevator when some woman ran up behind me and said jokingly, "Oh Karen, you're going home! Don't you think you should wait for your baby!" I've never forgotten those words.

The second type of loss we treat is spontaneous abortion. A

mother who has experienced multiple miscarriages told us this:

> "You can always have a baby." After the second miscarriage I just didn't want to hear this anymore. I wasn't having any trouble getting pregnant, but I wasn't leaving the hospital with a baby.

While the loss of a fetus in the early stages of development is generally considered more common and less traumatic than other forms of infant death, the failure to recognize the reality and seriousness of the loss to the mother is a serious error. These mothers feel their loss, a loss that occurs, many times, in a series of unsuccessful pregnancies that leaves them with feelings of failure as a mother, wife, and woman. Such feelings were described by one mother in her interview:

> I really didn't think I had that strong of an attachment to the baby. It just seemed like it was a bad pregnancy to start with because there was so much bleeding and everything. I felt sure that I could get pregnant again and everything would be fine. But I do remember thinking, what if it happens again? What if there's something really wrong with me? What if I continue to have this problem? I did get pregnant again — twice — and miscarried both times. I wanted to isolate myself from the world! Every time we went somewhere and even when I was with my husband, I had the feeling that everyone was thinking — "There is the world's biggest failure!"

Research has demonstrated that the loss of even a three-month-old fetus can have serious emotional and psychological consequences for the mother. The grief in some cases is resolved quickly; in others, it persists for long periods of time. The point is the mother has lost her baby, the most important thing in her life. This fact should be recognized and treated accordingly.

Since the actual miscarriage usually occurs prior to admission to the hospital, the staff tends to be less emotionally involved in this than in other types of loss. The common surgical procedure, dilation and curretage (D and C), does not really indicate the seriousness of the situation; that is, it underemphasizes the psychological and emotional stress felt by the mother.

Many women who experience miscarriages have few problems with grief resolution, particularly when they already have children. Their initial emotional response may be as great as in other cases, but the length of the grieving process is usually shorter and the resolution more complete. In such instances, the mother moves quickly through the stages of grief, accepts her loss, and, when given the go-ahead from the physician, attempts and usually completes another pregnancy. A few remnants of shadow grief may sometimes remain but this is usually not the case.

Unfortunately, the process is not always this simple. A miscarriage during the first pregnancy may have numerous repercussions. The mother who loses her first baby may experience feelings of guilt (What did I do?), failure (What's wrong with me?), concern about future pregnancy (Can I ever have children?), and fear (What if it happens again?). For many women these fears materialize since it is not unusual for them to experience two, three, four, and even five successive miscarriages. Their thoughts and fears are intensified and must be handled carefully.

We believe these cases should be approached in the same manner as any other infant death. The mother should have a sensitive ear available, someone to whom she can express her grief, and in no case should the reality or importance of her loss be underestimated. Many times well-intentioned messages may indeed do just that, as the following examples indicate: "Maybe you just weren't meant to have babies," "There are so many parentless children, why don't you just adopt one?" "Sometimes these things happen for the best."

Quite obviously, the motives behind each of these messages were either less than adequately expressed or the seriousness of the loss to the mother was underestimated. In each case the words lack empathy, and the mother will always remember them.

The third type of loss we deal with is the neonatal death. Two comments from mothers were these:

> I was optimistic on the surface, but I think deep down I didn't want to let myself get too hopeful. I wasn't dumb — I realized a six-months baby had little chance, but it was like you want to block that part out and grab on to the two percent or whatever chance they told you — that was what you had to cling to.

> There were all these people. The worst thing I can remember was everyone telling me to "perk up, it's all right. Forget it, you can have another baby." But you see, it wasn't all right, I didn't want another baby, I wanted that one.

One of the most tragic types of infant death is that which occurs within the first few hours, days, or weeks after birth. After an apparently successful pregnancy, normal labor, and delivery, the mother is confronted with the news that her infant has been fatally maldeveloped, that it is afflicted with one of several "high risk" neonatal diseases, or that it is the victim of birth trauma.

To some extent a mother faced with the impending death of a newborn infant passes through the same period of preparation for the eventual death as does the mother of a stillborn child. She waits; she denies; she grieves. Unlike the stillbirth, her child is alive; it has a definite identity and, however slim the odds, possesses a chance for survival. The mother feels helpless. ("There is nothing I can do"), responsible ("I should be able to do something besides lie here"), guilt ("What did I do?" "Do I have 'bad genes'?" "Was it the medicine I took?"), hope ("I know he'll be O.K."), and bitterness ("Why did this have to happen to me?").

During this "waiting period" the staff, particularly the nursing staff, can provide the mother with reassurance. They should allow her to cry; they must be patient with her anger; and they should give factual information regarding the nature of the problem. Where the situation permits, she should be allowed maximum contact with her child. While holding the baby is sometimes complicated by life-sustaining equipment, the opportunity should be provided if at all possible. Certainly on only very rare occasions should the mother be prohibited from seeing her child. Even in the case of malformation, the deformity may not be as bad as the mother might imagine it to be were she not permitted to see the child. As long as she is prepared for what she will see and for the feelings she might experience, most women will manage to handle the situation. A comparison of the following two situations illustrates this point. One mother said:

> I wasn't prepared for it — no one talked about it to me, not at all . . . . I realized that when I saw how beat up the baby was; he was really bruised. I felt just terrible because I thought I was the cause. After I saw that, all I could think about was how selfish I was. I felt very guilty after I saw how beat up he was. No one told me that it was rather common, no one told me anything, and I was totally unprepared for what I saw.

Another said:

> Even though he was a "waterhead," they handled the situation very well. The nurse explained to me all about this problem and prepared me for it. Even though it was a shock, I'm glad I saw him. If nothing else I gained a real understanding of other mothers who are faced with the same problem.

It is quite common for a mother, denied the right to at least see her child, to develop very negative and angry feelings toward the staff, perhaps justifiably so. As one woman related:

> They held my baby, they saw her, they simply didn't have the right to tell me I couldn't. After all, she was my baby.

Once death has occurred, the staff should be prepared for acute grief, and the mother should be given time with her infant, if she so desires. This is a time when the staff can simply make themselves available and avoid unnecessary conversation. A simple "I'm sorry, I understand your feelings" can be very comforting to the grieving mother. Many times, however, in attempts to help, the staff says all the wrong things. There appear to be standard phrases that many hospital personnel tend to fall back on, phrases that almost always convey an unvaried and insensitive message to the mother. As one woman said:

> Twice during the same day nurses told me that now I have a "little angel in heaven." They just didn't realize that I didn't want an angel in heaven; I wanted a baby to hold and love!

Another woman encountered a second "standard" phrase:

> All I would hear was, "Honey, you are young and healthy. You can have other babies." I didn't want other babies, I wanted that one.

Finally, there is the usual "Try to forget that baby." "Put this behind you." However, there will be no forgetting. The memory will live for many years.

During this period the nurse also may shed tears. Often a calm, cool, stoic approach may be interpreted as a lack of concern or understanding by the mother; on the other hand, tears say "I understand," "I feel for you," and "I also feel the hurt." The common belief that "my tears will only serve to upset the mother," may simply be a defense for the nurse. The mother is already upset, and other people's tears cannot deepen the hurt, as this mother's comments show:

> You have to accept it. That moment came to me when a nurse leaned over my bed, took my hand, told me he didn't survive, expressed her sorrow, and openly cried with me. I knew she cared, and to this day I just love her for it.

In many hospitals, photographs are taken of all newborn babies as a matter of routine. Such is not the case where perinatal death is involved. While it may sound rather unusual and to some even morbid, many mothers indicate a desire to have a picture of their dead child. This desire may not manifest itself until months or even years later. In the few cases where mothers do have a photo of their lost child, it is usually a cherished possession. We recommend that a photograph be taken of all babies — living and dead — and placed in the mother's hospital records. If she should desire it at a later date, the photo will be available. We are not suggesting that a photograph be forced upon her, but rather that it simply be made available to those who do want one.

Other items from the hospital which might be cherished in the future include the crib card, blanket, hospital bracelet, and a lock of the baby's hair. Each of these items will serve to keep the mother's memory of her child alive as time passes.

A final comment should be made concerning the responsibility of the hospital regarding birth lists. Most hospitals readily supply the names of new parents to photo services, diaper services, and so forth. Unfortunately, the names of parents whose babies do not live are not deleted. The parents return home to a barrage of unwanted phone calls and visitors. Improved interstaff communication could prevent this problem.

The final type of loss is Sudden Infant Death Syndrome (SIDS). Unlike other cases of infant death where the mother has been under the care of the hospital staff, the mother of a child who has succumbed to this unexpected disease has little, if any, contact with the hospital staff outside the emergency room. Instead, her first encounter is usually with emergency medical personnel, emergency room attendants, and law enforcement officers.

Because of the rapid sequence of events in Sudden Infant Death cases, hospital personnel have little time to develop a relationship that is conducive to the expression of grief. By the time the parents learn that the child is dead, they may have spent a total of two to four hours with the medical staff. We find, however, that communications during this waiting period can have a profound effect on the parents as they pass through the stages of grief. Consider the following account of a typical SIDS case:

A paramedic team responds to a call from a hysterical mother crying that something terrible has happened to her child. Upon entering the house they find that the mother is incoherent and unable to provide any information that would be useful for making a diagnosis. The father of the child is in a state of shock; he appears motionless and tearless. As they ask questions, both parents respond in a very confused manner, answering "I don't know" to simple questions. As the paramedics begin resuscitation attempts, a law enforcement officer arrives and begins to question the parents. The mother begins to cry and to cast blame upon herself. The officer approaches the child, makes note of the small trickle of blood about the mouth and nose, and again questions the parents. The child is rushed to the emergency room, the doors are quickly closed for examination and further attempts are made to revive the infant. After thirty minutes to an hour, the doors open; the physician questions the parents and then informs them that their baby has died. They are asked to sign autopsy papers and are perhaps questioned further; the funeral director arrives; friends and relatives wonder if the parents were to blame for the death. As we can see, this is a very rapid sequence of events.

Medical personnel need to be educated about Sudden Infant Death Syndrome and need to recognize the complete innocence on the part of the parents. Whereas many physicians may be knowledgeable about SIDS, they should realize that parents and other medical personnel may not be. When they encounter these cases and recognize them as such, they should approach the parents in a positive, tactful, and sympathetic manner. In most cases, the parents will be in severe shock, highly emotional, and experiencing many guilt feelings. These initial feelings of guilt may become lifelong if they are met with suspicious questioning or accusation. Such statements as: "How often did you check the baby?" "Have you dropped the baby?" "Have you ever hit the baby?" "Has anyone in the family been ill lately?" should be avoided if there is any reason to believe that the cause of death is SIDS. Such questions serve only to reinforce the parent's conviction that they are to blame for the child's condition.

Once the parents are aware that the baby is dead, they should not be ignored. With care and sensitivity the necessary information concerning the circumstances and causes of the death, along with some facts about SIDS, should be given to them. In addition, empathetic listening can be an unobtrusive means of gathering information from the parents concerning the details of the discovery of the child and at the same time allow for initial expression of sorrow, fear, and grief by the parents.

The parents should never be left alone at home or in the hospital corridor during the first critical hours. Touch and contact with someone else provides reassurance. Rather than admonishments "to be strong," or "You'll be O.K.," or "Everything will be all right," comments such as "You need not be strong," or "I understand your sadness and/or concern" imply that it is all right to express sorrow. Assuring the parent that "At least your child didn't suffer," or "You can have other babies" can in no way be beneficial.

Although parents faced with infant death of any kind need information related to their loss, it is especially important in the case of Sudden Infant Death Syndrome. Simple, basic facts regarding what is known and perhaps, more importantly, what is unknown about it, can go a long way in alleviating the fears and guilt the parents experience.

The parents should be given the name and phone number of the nearest SIDS parent group. These parents, having experienced

Sudden Infant Death themselves, can serve as a vital source of support in the months and years to follow. A partial list of parent groups is provided in a later section of this book.

NOTES

[1] "The Functions of Attitudes Toward Death," in *Death and Dying: Attitudes of Patient and Doctor* (New York: Group for the Advancement of Psychiatry, 1965), pp. 632-41.

[2] "Consequences of Death for Physicians, Nurses, and Hospitals," in *The Dying Patient,* ed. Orvill G. Brim, Jr., et. al. (New York: Russell Sage Foundation, 1970), pp. 171-90.

[3] "Care of the Family Who Has Lost a Newborn," *Post Graduate Medicine* 60 (December, 1976): 67-70.

[4] *Deaths of Man* (New York: Quadrangle, 1973).

[5] "A Clinical Study of Parental Response to Adolescent Death by Suicide with Recommendations for Approaching the Survirors," in *Proceedings of the Fourth International Conference for Suicide Prevention,* ed. Norman L. Farberow (Los Angeles: Delmar, 1968).

[6] "The Seriously Ill or Dying Child: Supporting the Patient and the Family," in *Management of the Dying Patient and His Family,* ed. Nathan Schnaper et. al. (New York: MSS Information Corp., 1974), pp. 187-96.

Saying Goodbye
And Looking Ahead

FUNERALS AND GRAVE VISITS

Although funerals are ordinarily taken for granted when an older person dies, certain problems develop when the deceased is a newborn or fetus. These problems generally revolve around three kinds of questions: (1) Who makes the arrangements? (2) What kind of arrangements are made? and (3) What is the "appropriate" mourning response from the parents concerning the loss?

When an elderly person dies, relatives are usually capable of handling the details. There are also certain socially acceptable, standard procedures to be followed. However, when a newborn infant or fetus dies, no such standard procedures exist. In fact, the single most important person in that infant's life — his or her mother — is usually recuperating in the hospital and many times is incapable of attending the services, let alone contributing to the arrangements.

Those individuals who are closest to the mother — her doctor, her husband, and/or her parents — often mistakenly assume that she would not want to be involved in making the plans, that her involvement would be too painful. Therefore the mother may be excluded altogether. Many times her husband becomes the one who shoulders the responsibility of making funeral arrangements. In fact, these responsibilities are usually thrust upon him — wanted or not — at a time when his own grief is overwhelming. In some cases, a grandparent of the child will assume the responsibility. While they do the best they can, again the result is less than satisfactory when the parents later evaluate the effort. The state of confusion that exists tends to cloud many important issues, and to lead to arrangements that are often less than satisfactory, particularly when viewed in retrospect.

The tendency of parents to avoid this unwanted, but necessary, task is understandable. It is tragic enough to undergo the anguish of the death of a wanted and dearly loved infant. Planning for its disposition only increases the hurt. While this responsibility is difficult enough under the best of circumstances, these cases present the worst circumstances. The birth that is anticipated with a sense of joy suddenly results in tragedy. The parents have little time to prepare themselves. Many parents and relatives who take the responsibility for making arrangements are usually not aware of the options available to them. Sometimes, in the case of early miscarriage, the hospital will take responsibility for disposal. The parents will be given the impression that this is not only the usual, but perhaps the only, procedure. The hospital does not explain alternatives.

Sometimes a well-meaning relative, in an effort to reduce the expense of burial, will request that a funeral home pick up the infant and dispose of it in a fitting manner. Under these circumstances, parents never really know what becomes of their infant. Initially it may not seem important, but later this question can plague them.

Anytime a parent is excluded from decisions pertaining to funeral arrangements, problems can develop, if not immediately, then certainly later on. Therefore, as difficult as it may be, the mother and father should participate in the preparations for the disposition of their infant. It is very important that whoever takes the responsibility for final arrangements respect the wants and needs of the parents. Communication between both parents, the funeral director, and/or a hospital representative is of utmost importance, reagardless of who ultimately makes the final arrangements. Excluding the parents, particularly the mother, for what is thought to save them further anguish, is not only unwise, but in the long run may cause resentment and bitter feelings. Even when the husband is involved, it is wise to consult with the mother.

Grandparents, who often mean well, can cause anguish for parents by insisting that they (the grandparents) take care of all arrangements. They assume they are doing a favor. However, what grandparents often fail to understand is that parents often are very sensitive to the feelings of others, particularly their close relatives. They will allow others the "privilege" of doing things for them which they should do for themselves. Making funeral arrangements is one of those things.

If two sets of grandparents are involved, the situation can become even more problematic. Consider the following statement from a young mother who lost her infant four hours after birth.

> Each set of grandparents wanted the baby in their family plot. Let me tell you, it was horrendous. No parent in their right mind wants to listen to that sort of thing when they are suffering such pain. They seemed to have no consideration for our feelings at all.

Thus, grandparents, who sincerely believe they have the best interests of their children at heart, unintentionally create additional problems for them. Relatives should remember that when it comes to offering help, the best help is sometimes no help, unless it is requested. This does not mean that close relatives should sit back and watch the parents struggle through their ordeal alone. It does mean, however, that they should be constantly aware of the confusion that initially surrounds the loss and of the fact that parents are often incapable of making rational decisions at these times. Yet making such decisions is something mother and father must face together, despite their irrationality. It is their responsibility and their privilege.

Nothing can quite compare to the anguish of a mother who has lost control of the final disposition of her infant and who realizes this when it is too late to change the situation. Some of the more common experiences of these mothers are revealed in the following stories. A mother who experienced a stillbirth had this to say:

> My husband made all the arrangements. He just went down and signed the papers and they picked up the baby and buried him. We did not have a funeral; the mortuary explained that that's how they did it. Some people

> might feel differently I suppose. I guess they wanted to make it as easy as possible, but I am beginning to have regrets that we weren't more involved.

This mother's reaction was rather mild. She did not recognize the implications of allowing the funeral home to make all the arrangements until several months after. She is now beginning to have doubts about this procedure, doubts that may well become more intense as time progresses.

The help and guidance offered by professionals or others is not always appropriate for every family. Another mother, whose premature infant died three days after birth, discusses the advice given to her:

> The big question was how to handle the arrangements. City burial or family plot? Whether to mourn or not to mourn? We consulted our rabbi, doctor, and several close family members. Under their "sound" advice we proceeded to do the very thing which for us was very wrong! We chose a city burial and did not mourn. Only weeks afterwards did I sense something was wrong. I was too upset, too depressed. My depression was out of proportion. I finally realized what was wrong, discussed it with my husband at length, and had our baby exhumed and reburied in the family plot. Only then was I able to come to terms with myself and her death.

Offering nonprofessional help can many times lead parents astray; offering advice, which is cheaper yet, can do the same. We are not suggesting that advice should never be given. What we are suggesting is that advice should be given only when the needs of the parents are considered and then only by someone who is knowledgeable about all the available options. Advice should never be based upon what you would like or upon what is common practice, but only upon what you honestly perceive the parents' needs to be. This may be difficult to determine. It requires consulting extensively with both parents, laying out all options, and choosing one which best fits their circumstances.

In some cases, established procedure is unsatisfactory, particularly if it calls for arrangements that the parents would prefer not to have. The following case, of a mother of stillborn twins, illustrates this problem:

> The administrator of the hospital came down and told one of the doctors who delivered me that we had to bury the babies — that we should make funeral arrangements. I thought a funeral was senseless because they were so tiny, they were so premature. I thought it was absolutely ridiculous to make us go through a funeral. I told my husband this, but he said he would take care of everything and that I shouldn't worry about it. Well, I had a hundred questions and he just kept brushing them aside. I could tell he wanted what I wanted — a simple burial without a funeral or service of any kind. I did not find out till later that the hospital administrator told him that a local funeral home offered a funeral as a "free service" to the community; they donated a casket and drove you to the cemetery along with your priest, or rabbi, for the service. My husband in all his grief had to go through all that alone. He went to the funeral home and then to the cemetery and watched them put those little caskets in the ground. He told me later that it was something he will never forget. He doesn't think anything will ever hurt him as badly as that did. It was a ridiculous practice, but we didn't know how to avoid it at the time.

This account is typical of well-meaning attempts to alleviate some of the pain involved in making preparations but which many times can have detrimental effects.

Because of her confinement to the hospital, the mother is often completely excluded from all aspects of the burial arrangements and funeral. Concerned relatives argue that it would be better if she did not participate, or that it would "definitely be too upsetting to her," and so on.

A third mother we interviewed, whose daughter was stillborn, said:

> All I heard was "Why torture yourself, let your husband take care of that!" Everybody kept telling me that it was "best" that I didn't attend.

This exclusion, well-meaning as it is, is tragic and should be avoided. The resentment and hatred that is generated in a mother who is excluded from the last rites of her infant can be devastating. Some strong-willed mothers do not allow this to happen, as depicted in the following case:

> They tried to keep me from going to the baby's funeral but I told them I was going if I had to crawl out of the window. I remember the funeral was at two o'clock and although I was still pretty weak I got dressed, went down the fire escape, took a cab, and attended my daughter's funeral! My doctor was furious and so was my husband, but I'll be darned if they were going to keep me from it. She was my daughter, and I wanted to see her laid to rest.

Regardless of her condition, or what other people think is "best for her," the mother should be given every chance to be a part of the final ceremony for her baby.

Closely related to the problem of who will make the final arrangements for the infant is the dilemma surrounding parental visits to the grave site in the weeks and months that follow the funeral. Grave visits often produce conflict for parents because of the mixed feelings that accompany these ventures. There seems to be no standard practice. Some mothers will make regular visits, particularly in the first few months after death. Others will not go at all. In fact, some have a strong aversion to cemetery visits. For example, a mother whose infant died four days after birth reported the following:

> I could not even go near the cemetery for a long time afterwards. I remember we had to go to a funeral of a distant relative and as we approached the cemetery I said to my husband, "Please don't go in there," and he said, "Why? We have to." I said, "I don't want to go in there," and he drove around the block twice and finally said "We won't go by the baby's grave, but we have to go to this funeral." I finally agreed and it was O.K. But I will never forget that horrible feeling of not wanting to go into that cemetery!

This response was common to many mothers, perhaps not with the same intensity of feeling, but the preference to avoid the grave site is real and understandable.

While many parents may experience different levels of anxiety over visiting the grave, for others grave visits can be therapeutic, helping the mother to dissipate her grief. The grave becomes an acceptable place to vent feelings. In some cases, however, the visit can serve to perpetuate pathological reactions, particularly in those instances where the mother has refused to accept the infant's demise. A mother whose infant died of pneumonia two weeks after birth is representative of this latter case. She told this story:

> Every time it would rain, I would go to the cemetery with an umbrella and hold it over the grave. I have asked myself over and over why I did this and I just cannot answer that question, although, I think it had something to do with wanting to protect him, as if I couldn't let him go! My husband, to this day, does not know about that part of my behavior.

Many times, if the mother has been excluded from funeral arrangements, the grave visit becomes an unsatisfactory venture for her, one she will probably try to avoid because the resting place may not be her choice. A rather common practice in some areas of the country is to bury the baby on top of another relative, thereby saving the expense of a separate grave. Where this was done, we found unsatisfactory reactions. Although this may indeed be more economical, from an emotional point of view it is less than satisfactory because it has the effect of doubling the pain and grief. Instead of one grave to visit, the mother now has two. A woman who gave birth to stillborn twins reports her feelings on this point:

> I was excluded from funeral arrangements and I did not go to the funeral. My husband made all the arrangements and buried the twins over my father. At the time I thought it was a good idea and so did my husband. However, I have only visited the grave twice and it was so painful. It's

> kind of a double hurt when I go because my dad was killed in a crash and it was hard for me to visit his grave before; now it's just impossible. There are now three people there whom I loved dearly. It wasn't nearly as painful to visit my dad's grave before; now I just can't do it at all. I wish now we would have made other arrangements for the twins.

Each mother must come to terms with the problems posed by burial. If she feels that having a grave or some other physical location where the child continues to "exist" would be too painful, she can select cremation as an alternative. Even after a hasty burial, which may later prove to be unsatisfactory, the infant can be exhumed, cremated, and the ashes scattered. Anxiety over visiting a cemetery is common. If a mother has these feelings, precautions can be taken either at the time of disposition or even later.

If a grave burial is desirable, such decisions should be made after the initial stages of shock and disorganization have passed. Temporary interment until more rational times prevail is one of the many options available, although few parents are aware of it.

THE SUBSEQUENT PREGNANCY

The loss of an infant is so traumatic that it can produce severe anxiety when another pregnancy is contemplated. It also can have a debilitating effect on subsequent pregnancies. Almost every mother we interviewed experienced anxiety; moreover, many encountered difficulties during their next pregnancy. Some were minor; many were severe. The trauma of losing an infant creates a strong sense of reticence and fear.

The big question the mother faces is, Will it happen again? Even her doctor cannot give the answer she so desperately wants to hear. Most women know that, at least in the case of miscarriages, the chances of miscarrying again are usually greater.

This fear can become so burdensome that some mothers cease their attempts to conceive and turn to adoption. This mother, whose first son died of hyaline membrane disease at the age of two weeks said:

> My husband and I have talked about having another but I have to say I'm really scared. I could never bear to go through that again. The thought of burying another baby is so frightening that I have actually become ill thinking about it. Therefore, we have decided to adopt. We believe this is the best course of action for us.

We can certainly imagine the feelings of those mothers who have suffered losses upon finding themselves faced with another pregnancy. Even if the subsequent pregnancy is desired, the fears and anxieties are still present. The mere suggestion that they may have to face the same hurt, the bitterness, the resentment, the sense of loss, and the loneliness becomes almost overpowering and can sometimes produce physiological effects that result in the very problems they so desperately hope to avoid.

These mothers plague their doctors with questions and concerns as they seek some kind of assurance that it will not happen again. They also look for some kind of recognition from their doctors that they are special people demanding special attention. Professionals, particularly the obstetrician and those who might have contact with the mother during her subsequent pregnancy, should be aware of these fears and should make attempts to handle these encounters in such a way as to offer maximum assistance and assurance.

These mothers experience subsequent pregnancies with ambivalence. Joy and happiness are certainly present but also immense anxiety and, in some cases, sheer terror. A mother who lost her five-week-old son to a heart defect talks about her reaction after the birth of her second son:

> I'll tell you, I was a wreck, a total and complete wreck! That poor man [her pediatrician], I drove him nuts! I did, I really did. How he put up

with me, I'll never know because I was a nervous wreck. I was afraid there was something wrong with him [her son] that he couldn't tell me about — all that stuff, you know. I must have talked to him everyday on the phone until he [her son] went in for his six-week checkup. Why that doctor didn't tell me to get lost, I'll never know.

The mother of a baby girl who died at birth recalls her feelings:

I was very happy and elated throughout the whole pregnancy, but at the same time I was filled with fears and anxieties. I drove the doctor crazy. I told him I ought to pay him twice! I was in there all the time. First of all I asked him to see me every three weeks and then I would spend, oh, forty-five minutes with him every time. I didn't realize that most of his patients didn't do that. He spent a lot of time listening to how I felt and it really helped, especially toward the end when I really got anxious.

Many mothers who have lost infants feel a strong desire to become pregnant again to replace the lost child. This feeling is quite natural. They believe that their loss can be ameliorated by substituting another baby for the one they lost. This is, for the most part, an individual decision. Generally, quick replacement should be discouraged. The mother needs adequate time to adjust to, and accept, her loss. If the mother has lost the child as a result of miscarriage, there may be a sound reason to postpone pregnancy. She may have physical problems that somehow contributed to the loss. An extended period of time between pregnancies allows a thorough investigation of any conditions that might have been, at least in part, responsible.

The psychological reaction to the loss also needs time to dissipate. It may not be necessary to postpone pregnancy or adoption until all evidence of grief disappears, since it may remain in shadow form for years. However, we believe it is necessary to postpone it for a sufficient length of time so that subsequent children will not be looked upon as substitutes or replacements. Having "replacement children" is an ill-advised practice. When parents produce a child that they consider as a replacement, the result is usually disastrous for both parent and child.

The substitute child creates significant adjustment problems for the parents, who find in this new child a living symbol of the one who died. Subsequently, their grief may become fixated; and they will be unable to completely resolve the grief associated with their first loss because the new child is a living reminder.

A mother who did not heed her doctor's advice and became pregnant within three months of the loss of her first child told us of the delayed pain she suffered by not completing her grief before the birth of her second child:

> When I became pregnant again, I was elated. I thought, at last, the hurt and the anguish would stop, and it did . . . for a while. But even before the baby was born, I was grieving again. I guess I really wasn't ready to go through a pregnancy so soon. I should have listened to my doctor.

Some mothers become very protective of themselves after the death of an infant. They often attempt to hold themselves aloof from the new child, to make as little emotional investment as is possible in the child. They do this out of fear that the same or similar circumstances will occur again, and they protect themselves from hurt that was thrust upon them the first time. Some mothers refuse to see or hold the new baby until it receives a clean bill of health. Sometimes problems do occur a second or even a third time, and mothers will completely withdraw from all contact with the infant until the problems have been resolved.

This woman, whose first child died at birth, discusses her reaction to her second daughter, born prematurely with hyaline membrane disease:

> She was sent to Children's Hospital when she was born. I did not see her nor did I want to. She wasn't very critical but just the reenactment of coming home without a baby brought back all those horrible feelings. I

took the planters out of her room; took all the baby clothes and other things, put them in the room and closed the door. It was like I was trying to push it all out of my mind. I finally had to sit myself down and say, now wait a minute, what are you doing here? She is not critical; she is coming home. I then opened the door, put the plants back and laid out all the baby things again. It was really peculiar while it lasted.

Another woman we interviewed, whose son died a week after birth, said:

When John was born, almost two years after we lost Mike (our first), there was a problem with his breathing. The doctor told me this almost immediately and my first reaction was that I just didn't want to see him. My husband understood, I think, but my parents did not. I just couldn't bear the thought of seeing him only to have him die like Michael.

In addition to fears that surround the actual pregnancy and birth, strong feelings of overprotection often surface after the new infant is brought home and begins to be integrated into the family. Many times the mother's concern for the welfare of the child overshadows common sense and creates problems of adjustment for both the child and mother. This mother discusses her second son:

I would not let him out of my sight. In fact, I didn't even want to send him to nursery school. I was just going to keep him right there next to me. . . . But then I realized that that wasn't such a hot idea, so I let him go, but I had some very anxious moments for a while.

Another woman spoke of her overprotectiveness with her second daughter:

Did I overprotect? Let me tell you, Janet didn't leave the backyard until she was three years old. Her feet never touched the ground until she was a year old! Yes, I definitely overprotected her. In fact, I'm still overprotective and Janet is fifteen now. I think the hardest thing is the anticipation that it could happen again, and you know you just couldn't go through it again, so you have a tendency to be a little overcareful . . . a little overprotective.

A woman whose first son died at birth — as a result of loss of blood and lack of oxygen due to an excessively short cord — described her reactions after the successful delivery of her second son:

> When Tommy was born, it really didn't help as much as I thought it would. I had severe depression after his birth. It was as if I had bottled everything up. I couldn't eat or sleep and on top of it, I could not take my eyes off Tommy; I was absolutely terrified he was going to die!

The fears that accompany these subsequent pregnancies are great and the tendency to overprotect the new child is probably quite natural. Mothers and fathers need guidance at this point. They need assurance that the feelings they are experiencing are normal, and they need help and assistance in dealing with them.

Although the subsequent pregnancy is fraught with difficulties, producing a healthy child goes a long way in helping resolve the intense grief of the first loss. Most women who had successfully given birth to another child told us that they knew that they had "made it," that they could deal successfully with whatever manifestations of grief remained, when that second child was born — and born healthy. Many felt that giving birth to a healthy baby was the most joyous moment of their lives. As this mother so aptly stated:

> The moment I heard a healthy cry, I cried, too! Not from sadness as it had been in the past, but from relief and happiness. It was the greatest moment of my life!

COMMUNITY RESPONSE

The topic of community response brings our study full circle. For the basic problem we deal with concerns the community's failure to respond appropriately to perinatal death. This is not to suggest that the community — all those people outside the immediate family who have an opportunity to respond to the loss — is cruel. The simple point is that infants have no real identity in the community. As important as they may be to their parents, they are, for the most part, unknown to the people who dwell around them. Thus we have the terrible situation of a mother, in what may be her deepest grief, living in a community that has no real understanding of her loss.

But within the problem itself there lies the solution — community awareness and support. Fortunately, during the past few years, parents who have experienced fetal and infant death, along with the professionals who encounter grieving parents, have come to recognize the need for outlets for grief and forums for its discussion. In many communities, parents and professionals have taken the initiative and have established active parent support groups. And the parent self-help support group is ideally suited to compensate for the lack of support from the larger community.

While there are several different types of support groups, the purpose underlying each of them is basically the same: to help parents come to grips with their loss. Different groups seek to accomplish this goal in different ways. Our purpose here is to present an overview of these support groups. In doing so, three basic questions about them will be addressed: What types are there and how do they function? How are they formed? And, how successful are they?

Though their basic objectives are very similar, support groups have different methods for accomplishing them. Through correspondence with support groups from around the world, we have found, with only slight variations, three basic types: (1) educational groups, (2) lay counseling groups, and (3) professionally guided groups. Many groups combine two, or all three, of these basic formats. Let us take a closer look at the objectives of the basic groups.

Educational Groups. The educational group operates on the premise that relevant information is the basic need of grieving parents. Self-help is facilitated by knowledge. As we have indicated throughout this book, the days, weeks, and months following the loss of a baby are filled with questions. Educational groups are designed to help grieving parents find the answers to their most pressing concerns.

One such group is HOPE (Helping Other Parents Endure), based in St. Louis. HOPE conducts a six-session course for grieving parents. The course can accommodate any number of couples; however, eight to ten seems to be the ideal class size.

The classes meet once a month over a six-month period. Each session is led by either a trained professional or by other parents who have had extensive training in relevant topics. Its objectives are summarized below in terms of what the group wishes to accomplish during each of the six sessions.

Session 1: The first session is devoted to introductions and experience-sharing. The members introduce themselves and describe their loss to the other class members. Through this session, class rapport is established and the parents come to realize that many of their experiences and feelings are quite normal.

Session 2: The second session is designed to help parents resolve numerous questions related to funerals, autopsies, medical problems, and so forth. They discuss the experiences they have had with these technical topics.

Session 3: Formal and helpful information is presented by outside professionals. The topic for session three is usually "the grief process." It is during this session that parents begin to identify with their own feelings. They gradually come to recognize that "I am like everyone else."

Session 4: This session deals exclusively with the stresses on marriage and is usually conducted by a professionally trained marriage counselor. This is a very useful session because it deals with problems that develop in every family having these kinds of experiences.

Session 5: This session focuses on sibling grief and is usually presented by a child psychologist. This is a useful session particularly for those with older children.

Session 6: The final session is called "graduation and spinoff." It is during this class that parents realize the affection they have developed for each other because they have shared a common devastating experience. This is probably the most important benefit derived from these sessions — the knowledge that others care, really care, about you and what you are experiencing.

Although they are not encouraged to do so, some graduates find these groups so beneficial and so satisfying that they resolve to informally continue their groups. Others who feel a strong urge to continue the service to those in need find alternative sources of training and become certified as group leaders for subsequent classes.

The HOPE groups offer a valuable service to families who often have nowhere else to turn for support at this time in their lives. HOPE fills an important need in any community and is a group easily created where there are families who recognize each other's losses and develop a will to do something about them.

The Lay Counseling Approach. There are a growing number of organizations across the country whose goal is to offer moral support and encouragement to parents, particularly mothers, who are experiencing grief due to perinatal loss. Trained lay counselors, who have themselves experienced fetal or infant death, offer a sensitive ear. By phone or by personal visits, these counselors are available at all hours to help grieving parents through their times of crisis. This approach is less formal than HOPE and is designed more for therapy than for education.

One of the most successful of these groups is AMEND (Aid to Mothers Experiencing Neonatal Death). AMEND, also based in St. Louis, is an offshoot of Lifeseekers, a voluntary organization whose members provide lifesaving equipment to hospitals and support obstetrical research through various fund-raising activities. The AMEND concept has since been adopted by groups throughout the United States and in several other countries.

There appear to be two essential ingredients to the success of lay counseling groups: (1) careful selection and training of the volunteer counselors, and (2) establishing credibility and a systematic referral system with the medical community. Obviously the first of these is necessary before the second is possible.

The most important element in an AMEND group is to have professionals conduct the training of the counselors, whether this is done by the members of a medical staff or a social services staff. The initial training consists of six sessions designed to allow prospective counselors to vent their own feelings, learn about grief, and become trained listeners. The topics of the six training sessions include: (1) introduction of individuals; loss of their infants; how to set limits; (2) relationship with doctors, nurses, and hospitals; (3) normal and abnormal grief; (4) the interview — listening to and responding to feelings; (5) how to deal with abnormal grief; how to make referrals; (6) review. Each session consists of lectures, discussion, and role playing. After completing this initial training program, the counselors are required to attend monthly meetings to discuss their counseling cases and to review procedures and methods. In addition to these formal training requirements, trained professionals are "on call" in case emergencies arise or if specific information is needed.

It is the policy of AMEND to always obtain the consent of the mother's physician before talking with her. This consent may also come from the pediatrician who treated the baby. These doctors must know that their patient is being counseled. A form letter, which gives permission to counsel a patient, is sent to the physician to sign and return. The letters are kept on file.

At no time do counselors deal with medical problems. If the mother has any medical questions concerning the death of her baby, she is encouraged to call her doctor and discuss these problems. Having a good doctor/patient relationship is stressed at all times.

Another function of AMEND is to provide information about the grief reaction to parents. A library available to parents and a supply of brochures and pamphlets for distribution serve this function.

Professionally Guided Small Groups. Another type of group that is gaining popularity is the professionally guided small group. This approach entails a small number of grieving parents (eight to twelve) meeting together on a regular basis, usually monthly, to simply discuss their grief experiences. The group usually is directed by a trained professional; however, parents who have, through their own grief resolution, gained expertise on the topic of grief sometimes serve as facilitators. Through the small group format, members share their experience and through topical discussions learn about grief and its attendant problems. Two organizations are representative of these types of groups: The Compassionate Friends and SHARE (Source of Help in Airing and

Resolving Experiences).

The Compassionate Friends is an international organization of bereaved parents, founded in London and presently consisting of chapters in England, Australia, Canada, and the United States. Its purpose is to promote and aid parents in the positive resolution of the grief experiences upon the deaths of their children, and to foster the physical and emotional health of bereaved parents and siblings.

The aims of the chapters are to offer support and friendship to any sorrowing parent; to listen with understanding and provide telephone friends who may be called at any time; to provide sharing groups, usually evening groups that meet monthly; to give information about the grieving process through its programs and library; and, to provide acquaintance with bereaved parents whose sorrow has softened and who have found fresh hope and strength for living.

The other group that fits this definition is SHARE. The original SHARE was founded at St. John's Hospital in Springfield, Illinois. The objectives of this group are as follows:

1. To show the Christian love and concern of St. John's Hospital and its personnel for parents experiencing loss of a newborn baby or miscarriage.

2. To recognize the need for expression of grief and related emotions that society generally denies these parents.

3. To further the hospital's philosophy of caring for the whole person and family beyond the hospital stay.

4. To provide these parents with a situation in which they can share their feelings about their loss, and therein find acceptance — if not always meaning. It is also an opportunity to express the love they had for their newborn in their compassion for others.

5. To aid parents in the positive resolution of the grief experienced at the death of their newborn.

6. To foster the physical and emotional health of the bereaved

parents, and indirectly, of the siblings.

We can see from these two groups that, whether international in scope or based in a single hospital, the goals are essentially the same. Each group is designed to provide social support and open channels of communication, the two most vital needs of grieving parents. It should be stressed that although participation in each of these types of groups may be therapeutic for the participant, therapy is not a stated purpose of the group.

Forming a Support Group. Regardless of the type, most groups are formed through the initiative and commitment of parents and/or professionals to whom fetal/infant death is an extremely important concern. Establishment of a continuing program is an enterprise that requires a great investment of both time and energy.

Whether the desired format is educational, lay counseling, or small group, and whether it is community- or hospital-based, the following process, suggested by SHARE, may be used as a basic guideline. Readers who might want to begin a group in their community are encouraged to contact several of the groups listed at the end of this book. Deviations from the SHARE suggestions should be made where they are appropriate, depending upon the desired format.

Since some direction is essential, a core group of several professional people should organize SHARE, set the atmosphere, and direct the meetings. In our experience we have found it helpful to have a core group of professionals, such as nurses, social workers, pastoral care staff and/or M.D.'s with sensitivity and communication skills. The core group members could rotate their attendance at meetings. By this method, continuity and security will be gained within the SHARE group. In selecting a core group, one factor is essential, and that is to have people who are dedicated to the group and who are willing to give freely of their time. As the group begins to form, it may be helpful to look at other self-help groups such as Alcoholics Anonymous, Make Today Count, etc.

The most direct way to get parents involved and interested in SHARE has been through personal contact; however, a small number of people respond to newspaper articles. These articles help keep the concept before the community, but they cannot communicate the personal concern and understanding the group is able to convey.

It is helpful to contact the newspapers serving the local area to announce a Community Information Meeting on the forming of a SHARE group. The editor of the Feature Section or Lifestyle Section will usually be sympathetic to the purpose of this self-help group and will print an article on newborn loss, bereavement, and SHARE. The article could focus on the grieving parents in the new group that is being formed to serve the area and should publish the names and telephone numbers of the committee members (core group), as well as the place and time of the meeting. Bereaved parents and members of the helping professions should be invited to attend.

Some of the people attending the Community Information Meeting will be looking for immediate help. Others, bereaved some time ago, will want to help form the group. Hopefully, some members of the helping professions will come to learn about and/or be involved with this group. Some groups may choose to gather a nucleus of bereaved parents and meet among themselves for awhile and then expand as the group feels comfortable in doing so.

In organizing a SHARE group, careful consideration should be given to the following areas: The meeting place should be accessible, with ample parking space and a pleasant atmosphere. The sponsoring institution (if any) may have a meeting room. Community centers, the local "Y," or a church or synagogue may also be appropriate. Some people have been concerned about having parents return to the hospital — the place where their newborn died, but it can be a forward step in resolving their grief for them to go back. If meetings are held in the hospital, they should be held in the same room every time, and they should be well away from the maternity or gynecology nursing units.

Groups should establish a certain hour for regular meetings, such as the first Friday of each month at 8:00 P.M. One morning meeting and one evening meeting each month is helpful to provide for parents working on different shifts.

A permanent mailing address, convenient for the committee members, should be established. This may be a P. O. box number, church, public building, or other institution that would receive mail on behalf of SHARE, or the home address of a committee member. A hospital address is particularly appropriate, since someone is apt to be available at all times.

One or more persons who will serve as contacts for the group should have their telephone numbers listed on the brochures, calling cards, and other materials used by the group. People seem to phone more readily than write. When financially possible, a listing in the local phone book is worthwhile.

There are no membership dues or fees. St. John's Hospital, for example, has provided a meeting place for the Springfield group and has given other support as well. Some donations have been received. Southern Illinois University School of Medicine has helped with educational aspects such as videotaping. Community service organizations may assist with other funding.

While there is no concrete data, there are several indicators that parent support groups in many communities have been very successful. It seems to make no difference which basic format is used. Each has an ample number of clients. HOPE, as an educational group, conducts classes for twenty people on a monthly basis; SHARE meetings are regularly attended; and AMEND chapters are continually training new counselors to meet an ever-increasing demand for their services.

Another indication of success is the longevity of the group. Rather than a one-time occurrence, these groups often become fixtures in the community. Several have lifespans of over ten years. Some have become recipients of government grants; others have become integral parts of hospital programs.

The greatest sign of their success has been their acceptance by the medical community. Groups such as SHARE and AMEND have been fully accepted in their communities and have proven themselves to doctors, nurses, and social workers. Evidence of their credibility is seen in the large number of referrals they get from the medical community.

Grieving parents need support and outlets for their fears and concerns. In many communities they are finding help. The future is indeed bright for the proliferation of support groups. Therefore, the future is equally bright for bereaved parents.

From Parent To Parent

Throughout this book, the parent's response to the loss of an infant has been discussed through the eyes of two professionals. During the past several years, numerous parents have, through a number of support group newsletters, offered their own experiences and suggestions for coping with infant loss. Borrowing from the Compassionate Friends' motto, "He best understands who has felt the pain," we offer this final chapter as a collection of information, suggestions, and advice from those who have been there — parents who have suffered losses.

GRIEF

Grief is a syndrome of feelings and emotions that vary from person to person. Yet, there are characteristics of grief that many parents share. The following three selections attempt to identify those characteristics and, in addition, answer some common questions of grieving parents, such as: Are my feelings and thoughts abnormal? How do other people respond to such a loss? What are my needs during this time of grief? How do I get through this?

Characteristics of Grief

Grief is serious. Like a serious physical wound, grief is a serious wound to our psyche. We need to be cognizant of this psychic wound and treat it as carefully and with as much concern as we would treat the physical amputation of an arm or leg, realizing that although we can heal completely, we will never forget the pain.

Grief is accumulative. Many who are bereaved are dealing not only with the grief of their child's death, but with many accumulated lesser griefs, such as moving, loss of close friends, death of grandparents, or often the serious grief of divorce.

Grief cannot be hurried; it can be delayed. Parents should know it is "okay" to get stuck along the pathway through grief. You should try to keep your basic lifestyle as much the same as possible. It is important to avoid major changes such as changing houses or jobs, especially the first year.

Searching and yearning is a most difficult time of grieving. It is equally hard for those who are close to us as we are acutely sensitive to stimuli. Keeping pictures of your loved one displayed will be difficult for many, but it is essentially very helpful. Powerful feelings of anger at life and at an unjust God begin to emerge, and this is a time for questioning "Why?" and "Why me?"

It is normal to attach to a fetish at this time. Some will find great comfort in the feel and smell of a favorite belonging. Some will talk to, hold, or rock a toy, a blanket, a picture. It is reassuring to see these things as normal and helpful in getting the griever through this period of adjustment and in equating these actions to the "pillow talk" or "empty chair" therapy of the counselor's office.

Illusions are normal grief reactions for some. Those who experience them should enjoy the comfort of their experience and accept it as a normal part of grief adjustment.

Real physical pain is common among grievers. Often this will resemble the anguish the loved one experienced. Those who grieve may suffer changing eyesight, hearing problems, breathing difficulties, aching arms, and a terrible "pain" within the chest. These problems frequently send parents to their doctor or the hospital emergency room for a checkup and reassurance during times of grief.

Disorganization is painful and unpredictable. At first the griever may have been easily led by others. Suddenly the old patterns no longer work, he experiences a terrible sense of loss of direction with recurrent feelings of helplessness and lack of control. Now is the time to establish new patterns.

— Go out to dinner every Friday night for no particular

reason.

— Join a bridge club, exercise or swim class, or some other active group.

— Take up a new hobby such as bowling, volleyball, or painting.

Eventually the new patterns become comfortable, filling the voids and gaps, and leading to successful recovery. Exercise and physical activity are especially important at this time.

The Compassionate Friends
Aurora, Illinois

Responses to Grief

Because grief can be so painful and seem overwhelming, it frightens us. Many people worry whether they are grieving in the "right" way, and wonder if the feelings they have are natural. Most people who suffer a loss experience one or more of the following:

— Feel tightness in the throat or heaviness in the chest.
— Have an empty feeling in their stomachs and lose their appetites.
— Feel guilty at times and angry at others.
— Feel restless and look for activity but find it difficult to concentrate.
— Feel as though the loss isn't real, that it didn't actually happen.
— Sense the loved one's presence, like finding themselves expecting the person to walk in the door at the usual time, hearing their voice, or seeing their face.
— Wander aimlessly and forget and don't finish things they've started to do around the house.

— Have difficulty sleeping and dream of their loved one frequently.

— Experience an intense preoccupation with the life of the deceased.

— Assume mannerisms or traits of their loved one.

— Feel guilty or angry over things that happened or didn't happen in the relationship with the deceased.

— Feel intensely angry at the loved one for leaving them.

— Feel as though they need to take care of other people who seem uncomfortable around them by politely not talking about the feelings of loss.

— Need to tell and retell and remember things about the loved one and the experience of their death.

— Feel their mood change over the slightest things.

— Cry at unexpected times.

These are all natural and normal grief responses.

— The Compassionate Friends

What Do We Need During Grief?

TIME — Time alone and time with others whom you trust and who will listen when you need to talk. Months and years of time to feel and understand the feelings that go along with loss.

REST/EXERCISE/ NOURISHMENT/ DIVERSION — You may need *extra* amounts of things you needed before. Hot baths, afternoon naps, a trip, a "cause" to work for to help others — any of these may give you a lift. Grief is an exhausting process emotionally. You need to replenish yourself. Follow what feels healing to you and what connects you to the people and things you love.

SECURITY — Try to reduce or find help for financial or other stresses in your life. Allow yourself to be close to those you trust. Getting back into routine helps. You may need to allow yourself to do things at your own pace.

HOPE — You may find hope and comfort from those who have experienced a similar loss. Knowing some things that helped them, and realizing that they have recovered and time *does* help may give you hope that sometime in the future your grief will be less raw and painful.

CARING — Try to allow yourself to accept the expressions of caring from others even though they may be uneasy and awkward. Helping a friend or relative also suffering the same loss may bring a feeling of closeness with that person.

GOALS — For a while, it will seem that much of life is without meaning. At times like these, small goals are helpful.

Something to look forward to, like playing tennis with a friend next week, a movie tomorrow night, a trip next month, helps you get through the time in the immediate future. Living one day at a time is a rule of thumb. At first, don't be surprised if your enjoyment of these things isn't the same. This is normal. As time passes you may need to work on some longer range goals to give some structure and direction to your life. You may need guidance or counseling to help with this.

SMALL PLEASURES — Do not underestimate the healing effects of small pleasures as you are ready. Sunsets, a walk in the woods, a favorite food — all are small steps toward regaining your pleasure in life itself.

PERMISSION TO BACKSLIDE — Sometimes after a period of feeling good, we find ourselves back in the old feelings of extreme sadness, despair, or anger. This is often the nature of grief, up and down, and it may happen over and over for a time. It happens because as humans, we cannot take in all of the pain and the meaning of death at once. So we let it in a little at a time.

DRUGS ARE NOT
HELPFUL —
Even medication used to help people get through periods of shock under a physician's guidance may prolong and delay the necessary process of grieving. We cannot prevent or cure grief. The only way *out* is *through*.

Judith Herr, M.S.W.
Hilltop Hospice
Grand Junction, Colorado

GROWTH

Parents who lose a child can never go back to being the same people they were before. But, it is not necessary that they only *lose* a part of themselves; they may also *gain* from the experience. Gain a closer relationship with each other; gain a greater appreciation for the wonder of life; gain the realization of their own inner strength. The following selections deal with grief as a process of growth and describe what parents can expect during the later stages of grief.

Transforming Grief

Time alone will not heal grief. You have to deal with it, to work through it. In the process, you can actually transform grief into personal growth. You can become something more than you were. Here are fifteen lamps on the path, lights to walk by:

1. *Accept the grief.* Roll with the tides of it. Do not try to be "brave." Take time to cry. This also applies to men . . . strong men can and do cry.
2. *Talk about it.* Share your grief within the family. Do not try

to protect them by silence. Find a friend to talk to, someone who will listen without passing judgement. If possible, find someone who has experienced a similar sorrow. And talk often. If the friend tells you to "snap out of it," find another friend.

3. *Keep busy*. Do purposeful work that occupies the mind, but avoid frantic activity.

4. *Take care of yourself*. Bereavement can be a threat to your health. At the moment you may feel that you don't care. That will change. You are important — your life is valuable — care for it.

5. *Eat well*. At this time of emotional and physical depletion, your body needs good nourishment more than ever. If you can only pick at your food, a vitamin supplement might be helpful, but it will not fully make up for a poor diet. Be good to yourself.

6. *Exercise regularly*. Return to your old program or start one as soon as possible. Depression can be lightened a little by the biochemical changes brought about by exercise. And you will sleep better. An hour-long walk every day is ideal for many people.

7. *Get rid of imagined guilt*. You did the best you could at the time, all things considered. If you made mistakes, learn to accept that we are all imperfect. Only hindsight is twenty-twenty. If you are convinced that you have *real* guilt, consider professional or spiritual counseling. If you believe in God, a pastor can help you believe also in God's forgiveness.

8. *Accept your understanding of the death, for the time being*. You have probably asked "Why?" over and over and have finally realized that you will get no acceptable answer. But you probably have some small degree of understanding. Use that as your viewpoint until you are able to work up to another level of understanding.

9. *Join a group of others who are sorrowing*. Your old circle of friends may change. Even if it does not, you will need new friends who have been through your experience. Bereaved people sometimes form groups for friendship and sharing.

10. *Associate with old friends also.* This may be difficult. Some will be embarrassed by your presence, but they will get over it. If and when you can, talk and act naturally without avoiding the subject of your loss.

11. *Postpone major decisions.* For example, wait before deciding to sell your home or change jobs.

12. *Record your thoughts in a journal.* If you are inclined at all towards writing, it helps. Get your feelings out and record your progress.

13. *Turn grief into creative energy.* Find a way to help others. Helping to carry someone else's load is guaranteed to lighten your own. If you have writing ability, use it. Great literature has been written as a tribute to someone loved and lost.

14. *Take advantage of your religious affiliation, if you have one.* The Bible has much to say about sorrow. As time passes, you may find you are not so mad at God after all!

15. *Get professional help if needed.* Do not allow crippling grief to continue. There comes a time to stop crying and live again. Sometimes just a few sessions with a trained counselor will help you resolve the anger, guilt, and despair that keeps you from functioning.

Mary LaTour
The Compassionate Friends
Dallas, Texas

Stages of Growth

A long time ago, when someone explained the "stages of grief" and how I might expect myself to act, swearing was mentioned. Four letter words, such as "damn," "hell," and so on, do help to let off steam. Some of the four letter words are *bad* words. There are a lot of other four letter words that apply to grieving, and not all of these are bad:

R-A-G-E   Often there's a lot of rage involved in a child's death; this is greater in some circumstances than others. Physical activity helps to let it out; scream, make fudge and beat it by hand, exercise, smash cheap dishes or cardboard boxes, find some household clutter and rip up each paper. You come by your rage honestly. You need a way to express it.

T-E-A-R   Crying is a human reaction to hurt. "Big boys don't cry" is one of the major lies. We all need to be free to shed a tear for our own pain or for another's. Go ahead and cry. It's another way to let off some of the pressure.

H-E-A-L   This is a lot to ask. You can grow new skin on a scraped knee and it will be about as good as before. But a parent whose child has died is never again the same person.

W-O-R-K   Grieving is very hard work. See how tired the people are who are newly involved in this work. But it's work that must be done.

T-I-M-E   The calendar is an ally of work. As days go by, you learn ways to put a patch on your wound. You learn ways to cope and ways to deal with your hurt. With the passing of time, the pain becomes less sharp.

S-L-O-W   None of the work of grieving is fast. Don't expect yourself to accomplish it quickly. Just keep on working. There's no honest timetable. The part of the world that doesn't understand may want to hurry up and "get over it." Those who do understand know that at first it's a good hour, then a good day, eventually a good week. And there will be bad hours, days, weeks, in with the good. It's very slow work, grieving.

H-O-P-E   This is a good four letter word. Hope for a smile to cross your path, for a friend to reach out, for the determination to work your way through your grief. Your child would want you to smile and live again with joy. You may have to go out and hunt for the smile, or call the friend and do the reaching yourself. That's part of Hope — expecting a good return for your work.

<u>P-L-A-Y</u> Trying to have fun may seem more like work sometimes. You may not have the heart for it many days. But do at least try it. It's encouraging to others who care for you. Go to the party or family gathering. You may be quieter than you used to be. Those who care will understand. Drive your own car. Arrive late and leave early. Try it.

E-N-U-F for now. I'd like to L-A-F-F. Think I'll go read the funnies.

> Joan Schmidt
> The Compassionate Friends
> Central Jersey Chapter
> Old Bridge, New Jersey

You Know You're Making Progress When:

— You can remember your child with a smile.
— You realize the painful comments others make are made in ignorance.
— You can reach out to help someone else.
— You can stop dreading holidays.
— You can sit through a church service without crying.
— You can concentrate on something besides your child.
— You can find something to thank God for.
— You can be alone in your house without it bothering you.
— You can talk about what happened to your child without falling apart.
— You no longer feel you have to go to the cemetery every day or every week.
— You can tolerate the sound of a baby crying.
— You can find something to laugh about.

— You can drive by the hospital or that intersection without screaming.
— You no longer feel exhausted all the time.
— You can appreciate a sunset, the smell of newly mown grass, the pattern on a butterfly's wings.

The Compassionate Friends
Carmel/Indianapolis, Indiana

DEPRESSION

Depression is a common problem faced by all parents who have suffered the loss of an infant. With it come many emotional and physical problems. What is depression and how do we cope with it?

Depression is an emotional state associated with loss. It is a feeling of sadness that may lead to apathy and withdrawal. It has been described as "the last chapter of what's the use?"

The key symptom of severe depression is a feeling of deep, pervasive sadness and hopelessness that lasts for longer than two weeks. Other typical symptoms may be: loss of appetite, insomnia, inability to enjoy anything, anxious or restless behavior, apathy, preoccupation with thoughts of suicide or wishing to be dead, loss of interest in sex, difficulty in concentration and making decisions, poor memory, irritability, feelings of worthlessness, inability to cry even if one desperately needs and wants to, intense guilt, and withdrawal from friends and relatives. It is important for bereaved people not to become alarmed because everyone experiences some or all of these symptoms at some time. If six or more of these symptoms are severe and continue over an extended period of time (so that pain and problems outweigh pleasure much of the time) then it would be advisable to get professional help.

Other signs of depression may be: headaches, backaches, crying spells if there is a marked increase in frequency and duration, unusual self-criticism, pessimism, discouragement, neglect of appearance, gastro-intestinal problems, fatigue, greatly altered motivation for work, family responsibilities, and relationships, less laughter. The definition of depression is the "act of pressing down." The physical appearance is also "de-pressed," for example: little eye contact, shoulders slumped, head hung forward, lifeless voice, slow body movements, pale complexion, obvious lethargy. Severe depression can be immobilizing. A person may feel so bad that they "can't stand it." A depressed person lives in a world with little emotional satisfaction, either in self, activities, or in other people. Depressed people withdraw because being around others who are enjoying themselves makes the depressed person feel more isolated and unhappy.

Symptoms such as sleeping too much, overeating, excessive sex drive, irrational anger, smiling depression, and alcohol and drug abuse are all ways a person might attempt to mask or overcome an underlying depression. A number of somatic complaints for which there is no apparent cause may be due to depression instead of physical illness.

Change is one of the main causes of stress and consequent depression, especially sudden or disagreeable change. Change can turn lives upside down and for the bereaved, change is a fact of life. Too many or too drastic changes often result in depression. Refusal to accept one's own limitations or to accept the human condition are causes of depression.

Losses that one suffers in the present can trigger the memories of past losses along with their painful and troublesome emotions. Such emotional turmoil may lead to depression. Loss often precipitates angry feelings. If these feelings are not expressed openly, then they are turned inward and may become a factor of depression.

Reversing the force and momentum of depression is possible. It takes hard work and sometimes the help of a professional, but it is possible to alleviate depression. Working to change one's depressing and usually erroneous thoughts can lead to relief. Thoughts tend to govern moods. Straightening out one's thoughts often helps one's moods. Depression can be managed.

The self-esteem of a person in grief can be very low. At a workshop on bereavement, studies showed that based on a scale of one hundred, an average person's level of self-worth is measured to be in the seventies, whereas a grieving person's score is in the teens. This low self-esteem can be accompanied by feelings of worthlessness and dislike for oneself. These developments need to be identified and steps taken to rebuild one's feelings of worth.

Suggestions for Coping with Depression

1. Recognize that the major responsibility for alleviating depression lies with the depressed person. It is important to acknowledge the illness and be open to accepting help.

2. Understand the facts about depression (causes, types, treatments).

3. Recognize the symptoms.

4. Realize that depression serves a purpose. It is best to face it and work through it rather than avoid it.

5. Talk things over with an understanding friend or loved one. Communication is one factor that may help a person not to become severely depressed.

6. See a physician for a complete checkup and discussion of symptoms.

7. Redirect energy in more constructive channels so there is more pleasure in your life. Pleasure is a source of energy.

8. Take a break for a favorite activity, an evening out, a trip, etc.

9. Get some exercise to help work off bottled-up tension, relax, and sleep better (walk, tennis, aerobic dance, etc.).

10. Work on sorrow — lean into pain — realize and accept death. Allow yourself to experience the many feelings you get, such as anger, guilt, etc.

11. Express your feelings — let out anger by hitting a pillow, swimming, screaming, hitting a punching bag, crying.

12. Become involved with people. Do volunteer work; try to help other people.

13. Try to look at life more positively. Try not to expect that bad things will happen. Work that good will happen.

14. Avoid extra stress or big changes if possible.

15. Practice deep breathing to stimulate physical energy.

16. Remember that good nutrition is important for mental and physical health.

17. Read about depression to gain helpful insights.

18. Know where to get help.

19. Seek professional help if depression is severe or persistent. It will not be as debilitating or as enduring as it would if ignored or suffered alone.

20. Examine your feelings to figure out what's troubling you and what can be done.

21. Write down negative thoughts and sort through them for the ones that might be dealt with.

22. Consider yoga and meditation.

23. Depression has its roots in irrationality. Make a conscious effort to dispute erroneous thinking.

24. Acceptance of the loss and resultant depression makes it less painful.

25. If you feel guity, seek forgiveness. Find alternatives to self-punishment.

26. Attempt thinking pleasant thoughts for one minute. This may take practice but it is a helpful habit to cultivate.

27. For someone in a depression, it is important to remember that alcohol is itself a depressant.

28. Pamper and be gentle with yourself.

29. Hold on to hope — grief and depression management take time.

30. Replenish self-esteem. Try harder to like yourself. Treat yourself as you would a good friend. Be patient, encouraging, forgiving, etc.

31. Do something you do well, such as a hobby or special activity. Little accomplishments help you to rediscover your self-confidence.

32. Remember you have a choice; depression can be managed. It doesn't have to ruin your life.

Recommendations for Sleep

Insomnia often accompanies depression. Therefore we offer the following suggestions:

— Keep a notebook by your bed and write down your feelings when you can't sleep.

— Don't nap during the daytime.

— If you don't fall asleep right away, get up and do something before you try again.

— Set a definite time to go to sleep and to get up.

— Exercise daily.

— Take a bath and/or drink warm milk before retiring.

— Read light or interesting books (not the type that stir one up). This may get your mind off your insomnia or depression, plus aid drowsiness.

— Avoid colas, medications, coffees and teas which contain caffeine.

— Take time to unwind. Do not go to bed after a flurry of

activity, either mental or physical.
— Try to think pleasant, relaxing thoughts.

Hope for Bereaved
Syracuse, New York

Loneliness and How to Overcome It

Why are there times when a bereaved parent feels lonely even though surrounded by loving people and people the bereaved parent loves? Loneliness is the outgrowth of separation from one who has given meaning to life. Yes, other relationships offer meaning, but it is normal for the searing pain from the loss of one's child to supersede the pleasure from other relationships and experiences. Part of yourself had been invested in another person. When that person has died, in a sense you are lonely for a part of yourself that has been destroyed. At times you look around you and think that no one else is experiencing the pain you are feeling; no one else's world has been shattered. This self-centeredness is a natural part of the grief process. Do not deny it, but *do not hold on to it as a way of life*. Give yourself permission to accept help from others and then to reach out and help others. Although your child is not here to give continuity to your life, by having lived and having given purpose to your life, your child can be the bridge to your continuity with life as a thinking, loving, and active person.

Ruth Eiseman
The Compassionate Friends
Louisville, Kentucky

Crying

When your heart says "cry" but your mind says "don't," listen to your heart. It could be your pride, not your mind, that is saying don't cry, for tears are hard for one's pride to accept. Crying because your child has died does not mean you are not a strong person. Tears do not mean you are having problems with emotional instability. You are crying because you are hurt. You were in love with your child and now your child is dead. Not letting it out little by little through tears may mean you are bottling it all inside. Is this good? Next time your heart says "cry," listen to it! You'll feel better for it in the long run.

The Compassionate Friends
Niles, Ohio

REMEMBERING AND FORGETTING

Remembering and forgetting, holding on and letting go — these are concerns of many parents. From the Compassionate Friends' newsletters, we find the following two contributions; the first a very sensitive piece written by a bereaved father, the second some thoughts from Dr. Dennis Klass while addressing a group of parents:

How Can I Forget?

A few days after you were gone, my brother said it was better if I forgot, but:

How can I forget the night before you came, when your mama told me she was in labor and the minutes we counted between the contractions, the night class I had to go to and how I bragged you were on your way?

How can I forget early Thursday morning, your mama awakening me to say the contractions were five minutes apart, us dressing your sister to take her to the baby sitter's, and how excited I was when they rolled your mama into the emergency room?

How can I forget the doctor saying he could not get a heartbeat and asking for another doctor, the nurse's reassuring comment that "they could not get my son's heartbeat because he was turned wrong," or the worried look that came over your mama's face?

How can I forget the labor room nurse's comment that "this doesn't look good" when she broke your mother's water, the straight, quiet line that came from the fetal heart monitor when they hooked it to your little head, the numb feeling that came over me when the doctor said, "Let's go out into the hallway," and he said, "from all indications, the baby is dead," the pain on your mama's face as she blew out the urge to push and we told her the doctor's feelings?

How can I forget the phone calls to your aunt while they delivered you, the long minutes standing in the hallway waiting, the card the social worker held in her hand as she talked to me, which said, "TODD — STILLBORN"?

How can I forget your mama as they wheeled her out still unconscious, the doctor explaining that they tried, but you had been dead too long and that your mama was going to need a lot of support in the next few days?

How can I forget myself lying on the hospital bed crying, then your grandfather and uncle crying on the phone as we talked and prayed?

How can I forget the first time I saw you next to your mother as she was just coming to, and her comment that "she was a pretty baby," or the second time when I held you for about three minutes and my tears fell on tiny feet, and the last time I saw your body with my parents and brother in the morgue?

How can I forget crying in bed and your sister wanting to know what that noise was or the first time of many that your mama and daddy cried in each other's arms?

How can I forget you in your casket, how sweet your little hands looked, the three white roses we put over your hands — one from me, one from your mother, and one from your sister?

How can I forget picking up your casket and driving through the city to the airport with you on my lap, the flight to Mobile, and leaving you at the funeral home for the night?

How can I forget buying the plot of land at the foot of where my mother and father will be buried, the services and the flowers, the friends and relatives who were there?

How can I forget the autopsy report and the doctor saying, "There is no indication for why this incident occurred," his feeling that it was your large weight (9 lbs. 3 ozs.), or your mama's look at me as a baby in the next room started to cry as the doctor finished his report to us?

How can I forget returning to your grave after everyone had left, seeing the turtles in the nearby creek, and crying tears on the ground above you?

How can I forget ordering your gravestone marker, not visiting you for over two months after your burial, and then my tears falling on the little engraved girl on the headstone over your grave?

How can I forget all the diapers I won't get to change, all the sleepless nights I will miss since you are gone, and the joy of watching you grow that I won't have?

I can't forget you, Meggan, for you will always be a part of this family's life and I can't wait to hold my little girl again in heaven.

Walter Todd
The Compassionate Friends
St. Louis, Missouri

Holding On and Letting Go

It seems to me that the one thing I see with bereaved parents is that you have a problem in as much as you need, somehow, to let go of that child and yet I see at the same time you need very much to hold on to that child. What I'd like to think about a little bit is how do you let go and how do you hold on?

How do you let go of a child? What I see in the Compassionate Friends is people who let go by honestly facing the pain that that death and that separation has brought. We let go when we let ourselves cry, when we let the pain, the missing, the loneliness, the question of why . . . when we let that in and let that pain fill our whole life. What we are doing is letting go of the child and knowing that what we have in his place is pain. And when we know that pain we know we have let go. We feel the child torn loose from us.

We also let go when we look our world squarely in the face. When we see the world doesn't have our child in it, when we see the world is different, when we see that people are treating us differently, when we see people don't want to talk to us about it. When we look our world squarely in the face without our child, we've also let go because we know the world without our child.

And I think we let the child go when we, at some point, allow him to be a part of something bigger. For some of us that means to say, "O.K., God, he is yours. He's in Heaven." For others, that means when we look out at nature, when we look at the woods, when we look at the ground, and we say the child is part of that, that he no longer belongs just to me. He is part of something bigger. When we say that, we let go. That's a hard thing to do, but we have to let go of the child, because if we are to live as anything except as emotional cripples for the rest of our lives, we've got to know that our child died and is not coming back. That's a hard thing to do, but we do let go.

The other side of it is that we have to hold on to our child. We can't simply let him go as if he never existed. What I have seen in the

Compassionate Friends is that people learn how to hold on to the child, too.

The first way we hold on is in memory. We remember the child. Memory is making him part of our every day as if the child were simply in another city or away at school. Just as, at some point, the child would have left home and we wouldn't see him every day. It is the same with our child who is dead, we remember him when we see something and we let the memory come. When we're walking in the store and we see a toy that reminds us of him, or when we're walking down the street and we see a little kid with a snowsuit like his used to look, or we see a kid on a bike the color of his, we remember. That memory is there and when we really resolve our grief, the memory is still there and it's a memory that feels good. We can have good memories and hold on to that child.

Sometimes we hold on to our child by simply giving ourselves back to the pain of the child's death by reading old letters, going through the album, going to the grave, or going through his things again. I've noticed that many of you simply let the present go its own way and give yourselves to the memory of the child. That is a good, healthy way to hold on to the child, by immersing yourself in the past, by giving yourself over to the past. You don't long for it; you can give yourself and commit yourself to the past so that when that letting go and sliding back into the past is over, you can come up and say, "There, I was there. I don't need to do that again for awhile, though I will do it again sometime." We can let ourselves go and we can get that child back for a time, and that's holding on too.

I think the most profound way we keep our child is when we maintain the bonds with him by sharing with others what we have shared with the child. That is, as you know, the secret of the Compassionate Friends. There may be parts of ourselves we don't like. Nobody wishes ill for their children, but we sometimes failed. We were crabby when we shouldn't have been crabby. Sometimes we yelled when we should have been patient. O.K. I accept that. We didn't intend to do anything wrong. The best part of ourselves with the child was the giving. To have a child is to learn to give and to learn to love in a special way that doesn't expect anything back.

When we can learn to take the love we had for the child and turn it outward, turn it so that we're loving others — at first, other bereaved parents — that is a kind of caring. I've found that in the Compassionate Friends, people have learned to care about other people very much, because they know what the pain of loss is and they know what it can be like.

There is a song that Melvina Reynolds sings that says it: "Love is something that if you give it away, you end up having more." Just like the magic penny: "Hold it tight and you won't have any. Lend it, spend it, you'll have so many, it'll roll all over the floor."

I think it's like that. We have our child. We give to the world what we gave to our child. We can remember, we can immerse ourselves in the past, and we can love. In these ways our child evolves us.

> Dr. Dennis Klass
> The Compassionate Friends
> St. Louis, Missouri

GETTING THROUGH THE HOLIDAYS

Holiday time: the whole world seems consumed with tinsel and glitter, but those who grieve are only aware of the terrible hole in their hearts and in their lives. Knowing the intense pain of the holiday season, here are some helpful thoughts which other bereaved parents have shared, with the hope of making your holidays easier to handle.

We must realize that grieving persons have definite limitations: we do not function at normal capacity; therefore, we must re-evaluate our priorities and decide what is really meaningful for ourselves and our families.

1. We must decide what we can handle comfortably and let these needs be known to family, friends and relatives:
   — whether or not to talk about our child openly.
   — whether we can handle the responsibility of the family dinner, holiday parties, etc., or if we wish someone else to take over some of these traditional tasks.
   — whether we will stay here for the holidays, or choose to "run away" to a totally different holiday environment this year.

2. Don't be afraid to make changes; it really can make things less painful!
   — open presents Christmas Eve instead of Christmas morning.
   — have dinner at a different time.
   — attend a different church for your Christmas Eve service.
   — let the children take over decorating the tree, making cookies, etc.

3. Our greatest comfort may come in doing something for others; some parents feel they can acknowledge their loss more meaningfully by:
   — giving a gift in memory of our child.
   — donating the money we would have spent on our child's gift to a particular charity.
   — adopting a needy family for the holidays.
   — inviting a guest (foreign student, senior citizen, etc.) to share our festivities.

4. Whether it's greeting cards, holiday baking, putting up the tree, decorating outside, or having a big family dinner, ask these questions before making any decisions:
   — have I involved or considered my other children?
   — do I *really enjoy* doing this? Do *other* family members really enjoy doing this?

— is this a task that can be shared by other family members?
— would Christmas be Christmas without it?
5. How many stockings shall we hang? We may decide to:
  — put them all up.
  — hang no stockings at all.
  — put thoughts and feelings about our child on notes, and put them in that special stocking. Family members are free to read them. This provides a special opportunity for younger children to express their feelings.

One family burns a special candle on all their special days to quietly include their "absent" daughter. One mother buys a poinsettia for her home as a living memorial to her son for the holiday season; another mother always orders a bouquet of orange daisies.

Christmas shopping is definitely easier if you make the entire list out ahead of time. Then, when one of those "good days" comes along, you can get your shopping done quickly and with less confusion.

If the thought of sending holiday cards is simply too exhausting, yet you discover that some of your friends are still unaware of your child's death, try this suggestion: enclose the simple little funeral service card inside the already bought greeting card. Parents have found the response from friends is most rewarding.

Remember to take one day at a time. Be realistic; recognize that you need to set limits and do only those things which are meaningful to yourself and your family. Know that whatever you choose to do this year, you may decide to handle things differently next year. Growth and change go hand in hand. And don't forget that comforting discovery that many parents have confirmed: the realization that when that "special day" arrives, it's truly not as bad — by any means — as we anticipated.

The Compassionate Friends
Fox Valley Chapter
Aurora, Illinois

RESOURCES

Groups

The following is a list of support groups to which parents may turn for personal help or for information on how to initiate a group in their own community. Several of these groups have chapters throughout the United States.

NATIONAL SUDDEN
   INFANT DEATH
   SYNDROME
   FOUNDATION
Two Metro Plaza
Suite 205
8240 Professional Place
Landover, Maryland 20785
(301) 459-3388

PARENTS OF
   PREMATURES
Houston Organization for
   Parent Education Inc.
3311 Richmond, Suite 330
Houston, Texas 77098
(713) 524-3089

SHARE
St. John's Hospital
800 East Carpenter Street
Springfield, Illinois 62702
(217) 544-6464 x 4500

AMEND
P. O. Box 2950
Hollywood, California 90028
(313) 271-1264

AMEND
4324 Berrywick Terrace
St. Louis, Missouri 63128

THE COMPASSIONATE
   FRIENDS, INC.
National Headquarters
P. O. Box 1347
Oak Brook, Illinois 60521

HOPE
P. O. Box 153
Florissant, Missouri 63032

HOPING
Sparrow Hospital
1215 East Michigan Avenue
Lansing, Michigan 48909

SUPPORT FOR BEREAVED
PARENTS
Houston Organization for
Parent Education
14207 Locke Lane
Houston, Texas 77077

KINDER-MOURN
6900 Percade Lane
Charlotte, North Carolina
28215

Further Reading: Perinatal Bereavement

Berezin, Nancy. *After A Loss in Pregnancy: Help for Families Affected by a Miscarriage, a Stillbirth, or the Loss of a Newborn.* Simon & Schuster, 1982.

Berg, Barbara J. *Nothing to Cry About.* Harper & Row, 1981.

Bordow, Joan. *The Ultimate Loss: Coping With the Death of a Child.* Beaufort Books, Inc., 1982.

Borg, Susan and Judith Lasker. *When Pregnancy Fails: Families Coping with Miscarriage, Stillbirth and Infant Death.* Beacon Press, 1981.

Campbell, Alla Bozarth. *Life is Goodbye, Life is Hello.* Compcare Publications, 1982.

Cohon, Marion Deutsche. *An Ambitious Sort of Grief.* Ide House, Temple University, 1983.

Colgrove, Melba. *How to Survive the Loss of a Love.* Bantam Books, 1976.

Donnelly, Katherine Fair. *Recovering From the Loss of a Child.* Macmillan, 1982.

Ewy, Donna and Rodger. *Death of a Dream*. E. P. Dutton, 1984.

Fischoff, Joseph and Noreen O'Brien Brohl. *Before and After My Child Died: A Collection of Parents' Experiences*. Emmons-Fairfield Publishing Co., 1981.

Friedman, Rochelle and Bonnie Gradstein. *Surviving Pregnancy Loss*. Little, Brown & Co., 1982.

Grollman, Earl A. *Living When a Loved One Has Died*. Beacon Press, 1977.

Ilse, Sherokee. *Empty Arms: A Guide to Help Parents and Loved Ones Cope With Miscarriage, Stillbirth and Neonatal Death*. Box 165, Long Lake, Minnesota 55356, 1982.

Jackson, Edgar N. *You and Your Grief*. Channel Press, 1962.

Jackson, Edgar N. *When Someone Dies*. Fortress Press, 1971.

Johnson, Joy and Marv. *Newborn Death*. Centering Corporation, 1982.

Kavanaugh, Robert. *Facing Death*. Penguin, 1974.

Katzwinkle, William. *Swimmer in the Secret Sea*. Avon, 1975.

Klaus, Marshall H. and John H. Kennel. *Maternal-Infant Bonding*. C. V. Mosby Co., 1976.

Kreeft, Peter J. *Love is Stronger than Death*. Harper & Row, 1979.

Kushner, Harold S. *When Bad Things Happen to Good People*. Schocken Books, 1981.

Landorf, Joyce. *Mourning Song*. Fleming H. Revell Co., 1974.

Manning, Doug. *Don't Take My Grief Away From Me*. Creative Marketing, Box 2433, Springfield, Illinois, 1981.

Miller, William A. *When Going to Pieces Holds You Together*. Augsburg, 1976.

Moffat, Mary J. *In the Midst of Winter: Selections from the Literature of Mourning*. Random House, 1982.

Montgomery, Herb and Mary. *Beyond Sorrow*. Winston Press, 1977.

Peppers, Larry G. and Ronald J. Knapp. *Motherhood and Mourning: Perinatal Loss*. Praeger Publishers, 1980.

Pizner, Hank and Christine O'Brien Palinski. *Coping With a Miscarriage*. Dial Press, 1979.

Price, Eugenia. *Getting Through the Night*. Dial Press, 1982.

Schiff, Harriet Sarnoff. *The Bereaved Parent*. Crown Publishers, 1977.

Smith, Arthur A. *Rachael*. Morehouse-Barlow, 1975.

Taylor, June. *But For Our Grief: A Look At How Comfort Comes*. Holman Publishing, 1977.

Tatelbaum, Judy. *The Courage to Grieve: Creative Living, Recovery, and Growth Through Grief*. Lippincott & Crowell, 1980.

129825